SPOOKY COCKTAILS

Copyright © 2025 by Cider Mill Press Book Publishers LLC.

This is an officially licensed book by Cider Mill Press Book Publishers LLC.

All rights reserved under the Pan-American and International Copyright Conventions.

No part of this book may be reproduced in whole or in part, scanned, photocopied, recorded, distributed in any printed or electronic form, or reproduced in any manner whatsoever, or by any information storage and retrieval system now known or hereafter invented, without express written permission of the publisher, except in the case of brief quotations in critical articles and reviews.

The scanning, uploading, and distribution of this book via the internet or via any other means without permission of the publisher is illegal and punishable by law. Please support authors' rights, and do not participate in or encourage piracy of copyrighted materials.

13-Digit ISBN: 978-1-40034-844-2

10-Digit ISBN: 1-4003-4844-7

This book may be ordered by mail from the publisher. Please include $5.99 for postage and handling. Please support your local bookseller first!

Books published by Cider Mill Press Book Publishers are available at special discounts for bulk purchases in the United States by corporations, institutions, and other organizations. For more information, please contact the publisher.

Cider Mill Press Book Publishers
"Where good books are ready for press"
501 Nelson Place
Nashville, Tennessee 37214
cidermillpress.com

Typography: Benguiat Pro ITC, CC Monstrosity, Cinder, Espiritu, Sofia Pro

Image Credits: Pages 4–12, 132–153, and 190–191 used under official license from Shutterstock. Pages 60–61 courtesy of Unsplash. Page 223 courtesy of Emily Tarkowski.

Printed in Malaysia

25 26 27 28 29 PJM 5 4 3 2 1

First Edition

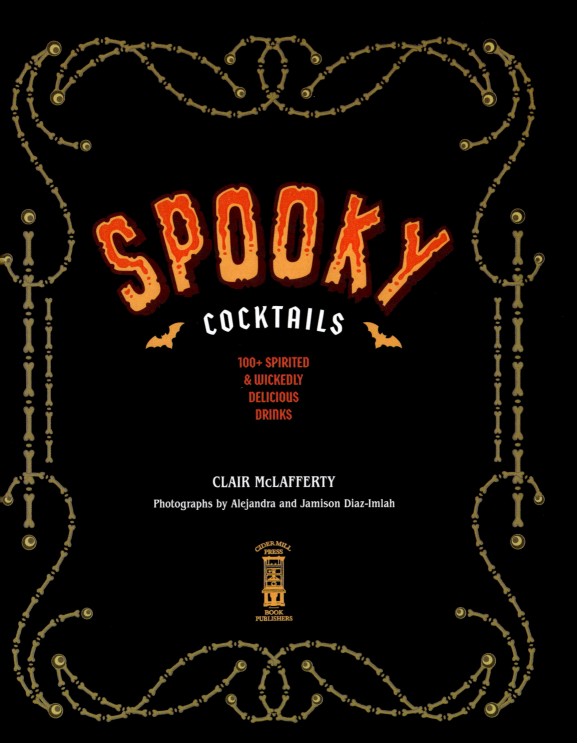

SPOOKY COCKTAILS

100+ SPIRITED & WICKEDLY DELICIOUS DRINKS

CLAIR McLAFFERTY

Photographs by Alejandra and Jamison Diaz-Imlah

CIDER MILL PRESS
BOOK PUBLISHERS

TO STEPHEN, NIKKI, AND TESSIE:
BECAUSE DOGS CAN *ALWAYS* SMELL GHOSTS.

CONTENTS

Introduction ☠ 7

Party with the Spirits ☠ 8

Notes on Potion Making ☠ 10

Mixing for a Crowd ☠ 11

Combatting Dark Wizardry ☠ 12

Scare-Free Drinking ☠ 13

Setting the Scene ☠ 17

Ghost Tours ☠ 63

Raising Hell ☠ 77

Rated R ☠ 101

Creature Feature ☠ 135

"Boo"ze-Free Drinks ☠ 173

Winter Campfire Tales ☠ 193

Index ☠ 219

INTRODUCTION

These days, spooky season starts August 1 or earlier and is basically a way of life. I love when the days start to cool down, leaves crunch underfoot, and a sweater and mug of tea brings the coziness inside. Add in the candy, costumes, football games, and spooky décor that come along with the change in temperature, and together, these things make autumn my favorite season.

The cocktails in this book capture the essence of at least one part of the season, whether embodying an unsettling name (page 77), warmth against the cold (page 193), a monster's lore (page 135), booze-free spooky occasions (page 173), or the things your favorite horror movie villain likes best (page 101). Many of these drinks fall under multiple categories, so this book's sections are our attempt at wrangling them into a taxonomy.

With all of this in mind, I have put together a guide for the cocktail recipes and any ingredients they might require (page 8), along with instructions to make stocking your bar less scary (page 13). Even when it's still ninety degrees outside, with the right drink and ambience, any gathering can summon the spirit of spooky season.

PARTY WITH THE SPIRITS

Building your bar from scratch can be a daunting task. Every week it seems, a new article details a slightly—or completely—different mix of products to perfect the process. The truth is a bit more complicated: having one bottle of each spirit does not necessarily mean that your bar is adequately stocked. Likewise, stocking only a few key bottles doesn't mean you'll be underprepared to be the best possible host.

Despite the widely held belief that liquor cannot spoil, exposure to heat, light, or air can change a bottle's flavor and color over time. To ensure that your bar stays fresh, start by buying what you know you like and will drink.

When you're first starting out, different spirits may speak to you personally. If you have a favorite cocktail, buy ingredients for that and learn to make it at home. Be sure that your measuring tools are quality assured—potion making is a precise art, much like baking (page 10). If the drink doesn't taste like what you were expecting, troubleshoot like a pro (page 12) to transform it into something even better.

Once you have mastered that first recipe at home, it's time to start trying new spells. These should be similar to the drink you have perfected, but maybe with a different syrup or liquor. For example, if you love a classic Daiquiri (page 144), try a Mojito (page 127). If an Old Fashioned (page 54) is more your speed, mix things up with a Sazerac (page 70).

When you get to the point where you want to explore recipes that would require buying multiple bottles, try the drink at a bar first. That way, if you don't like its effects, you haven't invested too much in supplies that will collect dust on the shelf. As much as a broader variety adds to the aesthetic, it may result in pouring bottles down the sink.

As a last note, investing once in high-quality liqueurs rather than buying a huge number of cheap bottles is the best use of your dollars. The flavors in the craft versions of these spirits will be richer and will deeply impact the resulting cocktails.

NOTES ON POTION MAKING

Mixing drinks is both a science and an art and is more comparable to baking than cooking. Recipes, as they are written, can go from delectable to unpalatable if they are even ¼ ounce off. For this reason, ensure that either your equipment is quality controlled or that you are focusing on drinks like the Emerald Gimlet (page 144) or Manhattan (page 108)—drinks that are straightforward, ratio-based tipples.

Likewise, as all good wizards know, random substitution is downright dangerous flavor-wise. For example, if you don't have absinthe, using pastis is fine in small quantities. But when making a drink like a Death in the Afternoon (page 84), the resulting impact will be huge, and the taste will differ greatly from that of the original creation.

MIXING FOR A CROWD

Some of the recipes are for large batches. Many of the others can be made at a larger scale, but to keep from turning your kitchen into a horror show, here are some tips when attempting larger quantities:

SIMPLE IS BEST. Anything containing dairy or egg may result in consistency issues or textural problems. Likewise, avoid recipes with muddled herbs or fruit, as these will likely be difficult to replicate at scale.

Multiply your recipe by the number of drinks you want to make. To make eight Manhattans (page 108), you would multiply 2 ounces of bourbon or rye, 1 ounce of sweet vermouth, and 2 dashes of bitters by 8. This calculation yields a recipe of 16 ounces (2 cups) of bourbon or rye, 8 ounces (1 cup) of sweet vermouth, and 16 dashes of bitters. Then add 1 ounce of water to account for the dilution that would have been added by stirring the individual drinks.

Since this mixture does not contain citrus or dairy and has a high alcohol content, it can be made days before the event and kept in the fridge. However, if the chosen recipe does contain citrus, make it the day of the party to avoid it turning bitter.

SPOOKY COCKTAILS 11

COMBATTING DARK WIZARDRY

Sometimes, your best attempts will go awry. Even the most skilled bartenders make mistakes, but the best of the best can fix them on the fly.

If the drink is too bitter, add the tiniest pinch of salt. Even at levels you cannot taste, salt suppresses bitterness and amps up the brightness on citrus.

If the drink is too sweet, add a dash or two of bitters. Although this won't change the sugar content, it will make the sweetness less pronounced. Citrus or floral bitters play well with citrusy cocktails, while aromatic bitters tend to do better with more booze-forward drinks.

If the drink is too alcohol-heavy, reshake or restir for a few seconds. The drink is likely slightly underdiluted. If this doesn't work, add a touch more sweetness. Sugar softens the alcoholic bite.

If the drink is crystal clear but calls for citrus, add citrus. Almost every drink that contains citrus appears slightly cloudy.

If the drink tastes watery, dump it out and try again. Your creation is unfortunately overdiluted and will need to be remixed.

SCARE-FREE DRINKING

Spooky season is the perfect time to pull out all the stops on impressive drink effects. The temptation to make a night-black cocktail or one that roils with cauldron smoke is strong, but misusing these ingredients can be extremely dangerous—and not in a fun way. As a result, these types of recipes aren't included in this book.

Although it renders drinks black as midnight and is almost tasteless, activated charcoal also absorbs many life-saving medications and renders their ingredients unavailable to the body even if they are taken hours before or after the charcoal. For a safer blackening agent, consider black food coloring (possibly paired with edible glitter) or squid ink.

Seething, smoking drinks are metal as heck. However, using dry ice to create this effect can leave behind pieces that can cause massive damage to the body. If ambience is the goal, consider placing the substance in small bowls with holes punched in the lids around the serving area. Alternatively, serve cocktails in smoking chambers.

Always, always clearly label drinks containing grapefruit. This common citrus interacts with medications that treat high blood pressure, abnormal heart rhythms, and other conditions.

Vintage glassware or old decanters of good brandy can be tempting to bring out for parties. However, glass and ceramics made before 1970 may contain lead that can seep into their contents. Likewise, unlined copper Moscow Mule mugs can leach metal into drinks. Consider, instead, using more modern recreations of these beauties.

For more information about these and other potential cocktail-related dangers, check out CocktailSafe.org.

SETTING THE SCENE

Spooky is a state of mind—but only with the right elements. The drinks in this section have names that are downright creepy, unsettling, or might be found in the scariest scene of a horror story. Many are classic cocktails, but a few are from modern mixologists. Perfect as the signature drink for a Halloween party, a summoning, or a random Tuesday, these drinks add an eerie edge to any event.

CAST A SPELL

ALABAZAM

Speak its name, and the charm will be complete. Just like any good spell, this drink combines familiar ingredients with an exciting new result.

1½ ounces cognac

½ ounce Cointreau

¼ ounce aromatic bitters, such as Angostura

¼ ounce lemon juice

¼ ounce Simple Syrup (see recipe)

☠ Shake all ingredients with ice. Strain into a chilled coupe glass.

SIMPLE SYRUP: Place 1 cup of sugar and 1 cup of water in a saucepan and bring to a boil, stirring to dissolve the sugar. Remove the pan form heat and let the syrup cool completely before using or storing.

THE DOILIES WON'T GET YOU

ARSENIC AND OLD LACE

This drink was named for the play that was the basis for a 1944 Cary Grant movie. But it also evokes the image of a house haunted by the living, perhaps plagued by the specter of lost love. No one wants to stay here overnight!

This spirit-forward yet floral cocktail was adapted from *Trader Vic's Bartender's Guide*. Imbibe with care, and use the coasters.

1½ ounces London dry gin

½ ounce absinthe

3 dashes crème de violette

3 dashes dry vermouth

Lemon twist, for garnish

💀 Mix gin, absinthe, crème de violette, and vermouth well with ice. Strain into a chilled cocktail glass and garnish with the lemon twist.

SHE'S ALWAYS WATCHING

BLOODY MARY

As the urban legend goes, if you say her name into a mirror enough times, her ghost appears. Given the gruesome tales of what comes next, you are likely safer saying "Bloody Mary" at a boozy brunch than to your reflection in the dark.

4 ounces tomato juice

2 ounces vodka

½ tablespoon lemon juice

½ teaspoon horseradish

1 dash Worcestershire sauce

3 dashes hot sauce, such as Tabasco

Salt and freshly ground pepper

1 celery stalk, skewer of olives, or other garnish of your choosing

☠ Shake all liquid ingredients well with ice. Strain into a chilled pint glass with a few ice cubes. Add salt and freshly ground pepper to taste, and garnish.

VARIATIONS: To end up with a **Bloody Maria**, use tequila instead of vodka; swap in gin for a **Red Snapper**; substitute absinthe for a **Bloody Fairy**; and nix the booze entirely to get a **Virgin Mary** (sometimes called a **Bloody Shame**). Get a **Green Mary** by using green tomato mix, a **Bloody Caesar** by subbing Clamato for the Bloody Mary mix, and a **Michelada** by substituting 12 ounces of beer for the vodka, sangrita for the Bloody Mary mix, and garnishing with a simple lime wedge. Many, many more named and unnamed variations on this cocktail exist.

SETTING THE SCENE

MICHELADA
See page 23

PICKED FOR A TOMB

CHRYSANTHEMUM

Few flowers are as closely associated with funerals as chrysanthemums. This cocktail is both spirit-forward and floral and thankfully does not share its namesake's cloying scent.

2 ounces dry vermouth

1 ounce Bénédictine

3 dashes absinthe

Orange twist, for garnish

💀 Mix vermouth, Bénédictine, and absinthe well with ice. Strain into a chilled cocktail glass, and garnish with the orange twist.

BE CAREFUL OUT THERE

DARK 'N' STORMY

Though it may derive its name from one of the best-known examples of poor writing, this cocktail is both spicy and deliciously simple.

2 ounces dark rum, such as Gosling's Black Seal Rum
3 to 5 ounces ginger beer
½ ounce lime juice
Lime wedge, for garnish

☠ Pour rum, ginger beer, and lime juice into a chilled Collins glass full of ice. Stir gently to combine, and garnish with the lime wedge.

VARIATIONS: Sub Old Tom gin for rum in a **Foghorn**. Swap in your spirit of choice to make a **Buck**. Swap vodka for rum and a copper mug for the Collins glass to make a **Moscow Mule**.

NOTE: Any liquor with citrus and ginger ale or ginger beer is part of a cocktail family called "the Buck." With gin, it is a **Gin Buck**. Bourbon makes it a **Bourbon Buck**, and so on.

> It was a dark and stormy night; the rain fell in torrents—except at occasional intervals, when it was checked by a violent gust of wind which swept up the streets (for it is in London that our scene lies), rattling along the housetops, and fiercely agitating the scanty flame of the lamps that struggled against the darkness.
>
> —the opening to *Paul Clifford*, by Edward Bulwer-Lytton

SETTING THE SCENE   29

SEPIA-TONED MONSTERS

FILMOGRAPH

Using this cocktail's name in conversation post-1907 may result in being treated like an ageless vampire trying to discuss modern technology. Its name evokes the villains, monsters, and stories from the silver screen.

To bring the cocktail recipe into the twenty-first century, the below recipe tweaks the original from *The Savoy Cocktail Book*. The original calls for equal parts sirop de citron (lemon syrup) and kola tonic. To lessen the sweetness and substitute one hard-to-find ingredient, the sirop has been replaced with lemon juice and a bit of Simple Syrup.

2 ounces brandy

¾ ounce lemon juice

¼ ounce Simple Syrup (see recipe on page 19)

¾ ounce kola tonic, such as Rose's

Candied Lemon Wheel (see recipe), for garnish

☠ Shake brandy, lemon, Simple Syrup, and kola tonic well with ice. Strain into a chilled cocktail glass, and garnish with the Candied Lemon Wheel.

NOTE: Kola Tonic is a non-alcoholic cordial that tastes similar to the base for soft drinks. It is typically caffeinated and may be ordered online.

CANDIED LEMON WHEELS: Wash two lemons well, and slice into thin rounds, about ⅛ inch thick. In a large saucepan, bring 1 cup granulated sugar, 1 cup water, and 2 tablespoons fresh lemon juice to a boil, and reduce to a simmer. Add lemon slices in a single layer. Simmer uncovered for 15 minutes, gently flipping at the halfway mark. Transfer to a cooling rack and let cool. Store in an airtight container in the fridge for up to two weeks.

THE MIST IS RISING

FOG CUTTER

As the fog rolls in, so does the sense that absolutely anything could be on the other side of the cloud bank. Driving a dark, curvy mountain road or even seeing a misty night outside your window triggers the human impulse to hunker down and try to get through the dark hours.

To cut through that unease, pour yourself a Fog Cutter. One of these classic tropical beverages may push away your fears, but be warned—drinking more than that may cloud your mind further.

2 ounces lemon juice

1½ ounces light rum

1 ounce brandy

½ ounce London dry gin

½ ounce orgeat

½ ounce sherry, for float

Mint sprig, for garnish

☠ Shake first five ingredients in a cocktail shaker well with ice. Strain into a chilled Collins glass (or tiki mug) filled with cubed ice. If needed, add additional ice to fill the glass. Float the sherry on top, and garnish with the mint sprig.

MAD MIXOLOGY: To keep the floated ingredient separate from the rest of the drink, slowly pour the measured quantity over the back of a spoon onto the surface of the drink.

SETTING THE SCENE

SLEEP TIGHT

HORROR HOTEL

Frederic Yarm, bartender, blogger, and author, Boston, MA

Hotels are anonymous places, many of which share generic décor and layouts. But haunted hotel rooms are a big attraction, perhaps prescisely because the presence of something otherworldly sets an otherwise generic place apart. The appeal inspired a Misfits song by the same name, which in turn inspired this bitter, smoky sipper.

1 ounce mezcal, such as Fidencio

½ ounce apple brandy, such as Laird's Bonded

½ ounce bitter vermouth, such as Punt e Mes

½ ounce apricot liqueur, such as Rothman & Winter

½ ounce Cynar

2 dashes Fee Brothers Whiskey Barrel-Aged Bitters (or Fee Brothers Old Fashion Aromatic Bitters)

Orange twist, for garnish

☠ Mix all liquid ingredients well with ice. Strain into a chilled coupe glass, and garnish with the orange twist.

FINAL WARD
See page 40

HOLD ON FOR THE RIDE OF YOUR LIFE

HORSE'S NECK

When a wild-eyed horse with its reins cut runs into town, everyone watching knows immediately that something nightmarish has happened offscreen. Whether it is man-made or otherworldly remains unknown, but something is out there.

However, this slightly sweet cocktail is more likely to revive one's senses after such a fright than cause one. Its name comes from the resemblance between the lemon peel's shape and the curve of a horse's neck—with or without a rider.

2 ounces bourbon

3 dashes aromatic bitters, such as Angostura

Ginger ale, to top

Peel of 1 lemon, carefully removed to remain intact

💀 Add bourbon and bitters to a chilled Collins glass and top with ice. Insert lemon peel so that it rounds the entire glass, and top with ginger ale.

SETTING THE SCENE

CHOOSE YOUR LAST WORDS WISELY

LAST WORD

Regardless of medium, the scariest stories often feature a final scene that calls its hopeful resolution into question—one last shot of a zombie escaping the perimeter, a monster stirring from apparent death, or a safe zone being overrun. These not only open the possibility of a sequel but also call the audience's safety into question. Like those moments, the flavors of the Last Word will linger with you. Have too many, and the drink will get the final say.

- ¾ ounce Green Chartreuse
- ¾ ounce lime juice
- ¾ ounce gin
- ¾ ounce maraschino liqueur

💀 Shake Chartreuse, lime juice, gin, and maraschino liqueur well with ice. Strain into a chilled coupe glass.

VARIATIONS: Substitute rye whiskey for gin and lemon juice for lime to make a **Final Ward**.

PRACTICALLY MAGIC

(MIDNIGHT) MARGARITAS

Since *Practical Magic* set the standard in 1998, few things have matched the witchy coolness of Midnight Margaritas. Our version of this potion calls for ingredients you can buy at the grocery store—no toe of frog or blind worm's sting required.

FROZEN

Lime wedge

Salt-rimmed glass

1½ ounces blanco tequila

1 ounce Cointreau

1 ounce lime juice

¼ ounce Agave Syrup (see recipe)

10 to 13 ounces pebble or crushed ice

💀 To rim the glass, pour salt onto a plate or rimming dish until the surface is covered. Run a lime wedge along the edge of the glass. Roll the glass onto the salt. Before pouring the drink, check the inside of the glass for salt. If any has fallen in, wipe it out.

💀 Blend all liquid ingredients with 1 cup ice in a blender carafe until smooth. Pour into your rimmed glass, put on Harry Nilsson's "Coconut," and drink up.

REGULAR

Lime wedge

Chilled, salt-rimmed glass

1½ ounces blanco tequila

¾ ounce orange liqueur, such as Cointreau

¾ ounce lime juice

💀 Rim the glass with salt as described to the left. Shake tequila, orange liqueur, and lime juice well with ice. Strain into a chilled, salt-rimmed glass.

VARIATION: Swap out cognac for tequila, lemon for lime (for both juice and garnish), and a sugared rim for salted to make a **Sidecar**.

AGAVE SYRUP: Mix 1 cup agave nectar and 1 cup hot water until agave is fully dissolved.

SETTING THE SCENE

FROZEN (MIDNIGHT) MARGARITA
See page 43

STRANGER THAN FICTION

MONKEY GLAND

In the not-so-distant past, pseudoscientists peddled the idea that grafting a specific type of monkey gland into the human body would increase the person's life-span and preserve their youth. Like many other aspects of "medicine" from this time, the very idea is horrific in and of itself. The drink named for it, however, is tasty and intriguing.

1½ ounces gin

1½ ounces orange juice

1 teaspoon grenadine

1 teaspoon Simple Syrup (see recipe on page 19)

1 teaspoon absinthe

☠ Shake all ingredients well with ice. Strain into a chilled coupe glass.

BLACK AS NIGHT

OBSIDIAN BUTTERFLY

Faith Sleeper, bar manager of Qui Qui in Washington, DC

This drink harnesses the power of squid ink to bring the darkness. Sleeper created the drink as an homage to the Aztec warrior and death goddess whose name translates to "obsidian butterfly" or "clawed butterfly."

1½ ounces reposado tequila, such as Don Julio

¾ ounce Cinnamon Agave Syrup (see recipe)

¾ ounce lime juice

½ ounce Amantillado sherry

⅛ barspoon squid ink

Lime wheel, for garnish

💀 Shake tequila, Cinnamon Agave Syrup, lime juice, sherry, and squid ink well with ice. Dump all shaker contents into a chilled skull mug and garnish with the lime wheel.

CINNAMON AGAVE SYRUP: Combine 2 cups agave nectar and 2 cups boiling water and stir until dissolved. Add cinnamon sticks and let steep for at least one hour, up to overnight. After one hour, move to the refrigerator. Remove cinnamon sticks after 12 hours maximum.

MOOR, PLEASE

SCOTCH MIST

Whether in broad daylight or with a midnight mist creeping in, the dips and hills of the Scottish Moors whisper of ancient secrets. This cocktail, named for the spookiest weather, is a utilitarian classic first published in 1930 in *The Savoy Cocktail Book*. It is also as variable as the area's weather: using different types of Scotch will wildly change this sipper's flavor composition.

1½ ounces Scotch whisky
Lemon twist, for garnish

💀 Fill a chilled rocks glass with crushed ice. Add Scotch and garnish with the lemon twist.

PLEASE DON'T TELL

THE SECRET COCKTAIL

Many of the euphemisms referring to even the most mundane secrets bring a hint of the macabre into the everyday. Whether you're keeping something under wraps, protecting the skeletons in your closet, or covering your tracks, knowledge of these things implies power.

In many supernatural tales, uncovering a secret is often the climax of the story. Likewise, this drink, modified from *Vintage Spirits and Forgotten Cocktails*, holds two secrets: first, it is better known as the **Pink Lady**. Second, its blush pink color belies a dry, complex flavor profile.

1 ounce London Dry gin

1 ounce applejack

¾ ounce lemon juice

½ ounce Simple Syrup (see recipe on page 19)

¼ ounce grenadine

1 small egg white

Maraschino cherry or brandied cherry, for garnish

☠ Shake all liquid ingredients well without ice. Add ice, and shake again until chilled through. Strain into a chilled cocktail glass, and garnish with the cherry.

MAD MIXOLOGY: Shaking without ice is a technique known as "dry shaking." Some bartenders swear by the reverse dry shake, in which you add ice up front, shake until chilled, strain out the ice, and then shake again without ice. Experiment and see which works best for you.

QUIET DOESN'T MEAN SAFE

SUBURBAN

Quiet neighborhoods are a staple of horror stories. At night, street after street of cookie-cutter houses is unsettling, and with a human or supernatural force in pursuit, the scene becomes disorienting and almost dangerous.

The Suburban, however, is only terrifying because of its strength. It is one of very few classic cocktails that combines whiskey, port, and rum, placing it halfway between an Old Fashioned and a Manhattan.

1½ ounces rye whiskey

½ ounce dark rum

½ ounce port

1 dash orange bitters, such as Regan's

1 dash aromatic bitters, such as Angostura

☠ Mix all ingredients well with ice. Strain into a chilled cocktail glass.

VARIATIONS: Substitute more rye whiskey for rum and port for ¼ ounce Demerara Syrup (see recipe) with a lemon twist garnish for an **Old Fashioned.** Patrick Bates would be proud.

DEMERARA SYRUP: Combine 2 cups Demerara sugar with 1 cup hot water. Stir until the sugar is completely dissolved.

UNPLEASANT TIMES

SUFFERING BASTARD

One horror movie trope is the infliction of suffering, physical or mental. The villain aims to cause pain because of past events. On nights when you've had a few too many, you might have been both the torturer and the tortured. This tipple was created to ease the pain of your hangover and is one of the few classic tiki drinks that does not contain rum. As with many libations in this category, drinker beware: downing too many turns a balm into a poison.

1 ounce London dry gin

1 ounce brandy

½ ounce lime juice

¼ ounce Demerara Syrup (see recipe on page 54)

2 dashes aromatic bitters, such as Angostura

4 ounces ginger beer, to top

Mint sprig, for garnish

💀 Shake all liquid ingredients except ginger beer well with ice. Strain into a Collins glass full of ice. Top with the ginger beer, and garnish with the mint sprig.

THINK PURE THOUGHTS

VIRGIN'S PRAYER

Cocktail-savvy readers may think this drink is a misnamed Maiden's Prayer. One look at the recipe, however, and you will likely change your mind. This fully separate—and potentially poisonous—cocktail first appears in the 1939 *The Gentleman's Companion*. In the original recipe, cracked cherry pits are left to infuse a nutty flavor into the drink.

Fun fact: that almondy flavor is a chemical called amygdalin, which the body processes as cyanide. This chemical is present in the seeds of all stone fruits (also known as drupes) and is quite soluble in alcohol. To avoid accidental poisonings, the recipe below has been reworked to give the same nutty flavor with nontoxic ingredients.

1½ ounces kirschwasser

1 ounce cherry brandy

¼ ounce maraschino liqueur

1 dash toasted almond bitters

☠ Combine all ingredients in a cocktail shaker. Add ice, and shake until chilled through, about 15 to 20 seconds. Strain into a snifter.

NOTE: Poison control recommends not eating the pits or seeds from various fruits, especially if they have been damaged. For more information, visit poison.org or cocktailsafe.org.

POISONER'S HANDBOOK: Many recipes for amaretto call for soaking apricot kernels in liquor. Apricots are also drupes and contain the same chemical. To render the chemical inert, amaretto producers bake the kernels and test the resulting seeds with lab equipment before infusion. Unless you can definitively prove that the amygdalin is dormant, we suggest using other definitively nontoxic ingredients to achieve that nutty flavor.

58   SPOOKY COCKTAILS

GHOST TOURS

No two lists agree exactly on which US cities are the most haunted. Some cities, however, show up time and again on many of the current lists. New Orleans, Louisiania; Savannah, Georgia; and San Francisco, California are generally agreed to be some of the most haunted. This section captures some of the drinks associated with the history or character of these cities.

EXPLOSIVE

Chatham Artillery Punch

Savannah's ghostly activity is often attributed to specific souls in specific houses. But as a port city during the slave trade, the destination for Sherman's March to the Sea, as well as the location for a yellow fever outbreak and the fire of 1820, the character of Savannah's haunting goes a bit deeper. Walking the cobblestone streets past nineteenth-century buildings under trees dripping with Spanish moss, one can feel the past all around.

It is not surprising that long-departed spirits hold on in some places. The city's best-known cocktail hails from the early 1800s, and was created by a local artillery unit. As with many other things, the recipe evolved into a slightly mellower, sweeter sip, but even in that form, the drink still packs a wallop.

Lemon Oleo Saccharum (see recipe)
1 (750 ml) bottle cognac
1 (750 ml) bottle bourbon
1 (750 ml) bottle Jamaican-style rum
3 bottles brut champagne, to top

💀 When you are ready to serve, fill a very large (2½ gallon or larger) punch bowl with cracked ice. Add the Lemon Oleo Saccharum, cognac, bourbon, and rum. Top with the three bottles of champagne.

LEMON OLEO SACCHARUM: Peel 12 lemons, getting as little of the pith as possible, then scrape or trim any remaining pith. Muddle the peels in a sturdy bowl or airtight container with 2 cups raw sugar. Cover and let sit for at least an hour at room temperature. Muddle again. Mix in 2 cups freshly squeezed and strained lemon juice. Stir until sugar is largely liquified, and strain into an empty, sterilized 750 mL bottle. Fill any remaining space with water, and refrigerate.

BATTEN THE HATCHES

HURRICANE

In New Orleans, hurricanes are an intense subject of conversation. The city sits below sea level, so the threat of a storm system is concerning. Pat O'Brien's, a local bar that has since expanded into a nationwide chain, lays claim to creating the cocktail of the same name in the 1940s. As with many other tipples, other origin stories exist, one claiming that the Hurricane Bar served a rum-based drink served in a hurricane glass during the 1939 New York World's Fair.

Whatever you believe, the recipe below will have your head spinning. Though the finished drink isn't as red as the mix sold by Pat O'Brien's, it is likely closer to what the locals were sipping in the 1940s.

2 ounces aged rum (or 1 ounce Jamaican-style rum and 1 ounce aged rum)

1 ounce passion fruit syrup or puree

1 ounce lemon juice

Orange wheel and maraschino cherries, for garnish

☠ Shake rum, passion fruit puree, and lemon juice well with ice. Strain into a chilled hurricane glass filled with crushed ice. Garnish with orange slice and maraschino cherries.

LIGHT AS A CLOUD

RAMOS GIN FIZZ

New Orleans's history is riddled with pirates, disease, enslavement, crime, and debauchery—an undeniable recipe for haunting. And that is not to mention its ties to voodoo and hoodoo.

As one of the city's most iconic drinks, the Ramos Gin Fizz is also one of the most difficult recipes to get right. Clocking in with eight ingredients and at least five minutes of shaking time, it is a drink that takes serious work. The result is a hauntingly beautiful beverage; it is light, sweet, and refreshing. But even at most places in the Big Easy, don't ask a bartender to make it during a busy night—they will likely say no.

1½ ounces Old Tom gin
1 ounce heavy cream
½ ounce Simple Syrup (see recipe on page 19)

½ ounce lemon juice
½ ounce lime juice
1 egg white

1 dash orange flower water
Club soda, to top
Orange twist, for garnish

💀 Shake all liquid ingredients except club soda well without ice. Add ice, and shake for at least 2 minutes. The tin may frost, but you can use a towel or gloves to continue shaking. Pour 1 inch of club soda into a chilled Collins glass. Strain the mixture into the glass. Continue topping gently with soda water until the head of foam peeks over the edge of the glass. Garnish with the orange twist and serve with a straw.

MAD MIXOLOGY: Some bartenders swear by removing the spring from their Hawthorne strainers and adding it to the shaker. Your mileage may vary.

SWEET AND DEADLY

SAZERAC

New Orleans shapeshifts when the sun goes down. The Spanish moss–covered trees go from elegant to otherworldly; streets go from mostly safe to not; and ghost stories told in daylight take on harder edges.

The Sazerac is also a shapeshifter. Originally, its recipe called for cognac instead of whiskey, but when an aphid plague chewed through European grape crops in the late nineteenth century, the substitution was made and has stuck since.

2 dashes absinthe

3 dashes Peychaud's Bitters

¼ ounce Simple Syrup (see recipe on page 19) or sugar cube

2 ounces rye whiskey

Lemon twist, for garnish

💀 Dash the absinthe into a chilled rocks glass. Roll the glass until coated, and discard excess. Add Simple Syrup and bitters to rinsed glass, or muddle the sugar cube with bitters and a small amount of water. Add whiskey and ice. Stir until chilled through, 15 to 20 seconds. Garnish with the lemon twist.

NOTE: As defined in 1806, a cocktail is "a stimulating liquor composed of spirits of any kind, sugar, water, and bitters." In those days, if you wanted this type of drink with whiskey, you ordered a Whiskey Cocktail, not an Old Fashioned (page 54). The drink was invented at a bar called the Sazerac House and was made using Sazerac de Forge et Fils cognac, so it was likely named for its base spirit.

BACK IN THE OLD SQUARE

VIEUX CARRÉ

As the French name for the French Quarter in New Orleans, this cocktail is a tribute to the city itself. Mixing traditional French ingredients with American whiskey and local bitters, the drink embodies the local culture with a complex, slightly herbal flavor. Like the city, the drink finishes with a quick, sweet bite, and its strength will quickly have you stumbling.

¾ **ounce rye whiskey**

¾ **ounce cognac**

¾ **ounce sweet vermouth**

1 teaspoon Bénédictine

2 dashes Peychaud's Bitters

2 dashes aromatic bitters, such as Angostura

Maraschino cherry, for garnish

☠ Mix liquid ingredients well with ice. Strain into a chilled rocks glass with a large cube, and garnish with the cherry.

VARIATIONS: Substitute Bénédictine for cognac for a total ¾ ounce, absinthe for the aromatic bitters, and a cocktail glass instead of the rocks glass to make a **Cocktail de la Louisiane**.

GLEAMING, TWINKLING

GOLD RUSH

With the discovery of gold in the Sierra Nevada foothills, San Francisco was transformed almost overnight from a small port town to a bustling city. In the transformation's aftermath, the results of overnight wealth, earthquakes and fires, as well as Alcatraz, have landed the city on many haunted destination lists.

The Gold Rush is a more modern entry in a cocktail family called The Sours. Despite several well-documented classic honey and lemon Sours (see Variations below), this recipe was not written down until 1999.

2 ounces bourbon whiskey
¾ ounce Honey Syrup (see recipe)
¾ ounce lemon juice

☠ Shake bourbon, Honey Syrup, and lemon juice well with ice. Strain into a chilled rocks glass with a large cube.

VARIATIONS: Substitute rum for a **Princess** or gin for a **Bee's Knees**.

HONEY SYRUP: Combine 1 cup honey with 1 cup hot water. Stir until the honey is incorporated.

RAISING HELL

These devilish drinks are perfect for the days (or nights) when you need to raise a little Cain. Named for death, hell, or even Beelezebub himself, the tipples in this section are sure to spice up your drinking with a taste of wickedness.

RED DEVIL,

BLUE DEVIL

Depending on who you ask, a blue devil is either a euphemism for depression or a member of a wickedly efficient French fighting unit from World War I. Though the slang definition has been around since the 1700s, this cocktail was first published in the 1930s. Since more cocktails are named for fighting forces than emotions, it is likely this cocktail was named for the French squadron.

1½ ounces London dry gin

¾ ounce lemon juice

½ ounce Simple Syrup (see recipe on page 19)

¼ ounce maraschino liqueur

2 drops blue food coloring

☠ Shake gin, lemon juice, Simple Syrup, maraschino liqueur, and blue food coloring with ice. Strain into a chilled coupe glass.

MAD MIXOLOGY: Food coloring is a safe and fun way to change beverages' color without impacting the drink's flavor. Some ingredients, like blue curaçao, already contain the color. Adding the food coloring yourself allows more control over the saturation of the pigment as well as the flavors of the drink itself.

ONE OR TWO REVIVE THE CORPSE...

Corpse Reviver No. 1

Although this cocktail and the Corpse Reviver No. 2 share a name and surprising strength, the similarities end there. This concoction is boozy, spirituous, and best sipped slowly, while the No. 2 is lighter, citrusy, and more refreshing. To properly balance its flavor, we suggest using a vermouth with a pronounced bitter component, such as Punt E Mes. If your sweet vermouth is from another producer, add 2 dashes aromatic bitters, such as Angostura, to balance it out (Combatting Dark Wizardry, page 12).

1 ounce Armagnac
1 ounce Calvados
1 ounce sweet vermouth, such as Punt e Mes
Maraschino cherry, for garnish

💀 Mix Armagnac, Calvados, and sweet vermouth well with ice. Strain into a chilled coupe glass, and garnish with the maraschino cherry.

... FOUR OR MORE TAKEN IN QUICK SUCCESSION WILL UNREVIVE THE CORPSE AGAIN

CORPSE REVIVER NO. 2

The drink's name stems from its origins as a hangover cure but may also hold a yet undiscovered power to vanquish zombies. We suggest sticking to tried and true methods for dealing with the supernatural, but when you're feeling like a corpse because of a hangover, this drink will help bring you back to life.

¾ **ounce London dry gin**

¾ **ounce Lillet Blanc or Cocchi Americano Bianco**

¾ **ounce orange liqueur, such as Cointreau**

¾ **ounce lemon juice**

1 dash absinthe

1 strip lemon peel, for garnish

☠ Shake gin, Lillet Blanc, orange liqueur, lemon juice, and absinthe well with ice. Strain into a chilled couple glass, and garnish with the lemon peel.

RAISING HELL 83

LE PETIT MORT DU JOUR

DEATH IN THE AFTERNOON

This cocktail is Earnest Hemingway's simple but wickedly strong contribution to cocktail history. Drink with caution.

1 ounce absinthe

4 to 5 ounces chilled champagne, to top

☠ Pour the absinthe into a chilled champagne flute. Slowly top with the champagne.

NOTE: Back in the early 1900s, absinthe was becoming one of the most popular drinks in Europe—so popular, in fact, that it was encroaching on French wine sales and inspiring bootleg production. Unscrupulous producers used toxic materials to mimic the flavor and visual qualities of absinthe, leading to a string of deaths, crimes, and reported hallucinations tied to the product.

The wine industry ran with these accounts, and many countries banned absinthe in the early 1900s. Roughly a century later, it was relegalized within the US in 2007. Some commercially available brands were actually reverse engineered using chemical spectrographic analysis on the contents of centuries-old bottles. Despite what your friends might have told you, real absinthe is available today.

HE'S IN THE DETAILS

DEVIL'S COCKTAIL

This low ABV sipper is just sweet enough to be crushable and just potent enough to be dangerous. While drinking these, do not stop to talk to strange folks standing at crossroads, and if you do, do not make any deals with them.

½ ounce tawny port
1½ ounces sweet vermouth
¼ to ½ ounce lemon juice

💀 Shake port, vermouth, and lemon juice with ice. Strain into a chilled cocktail glass.

HE GOES BY MANY NAMES

EL DIABLO

This devilish drink first appeared in a Trader Vic's recipe book sometime in the 1940s and is one of the only classic tequila cocktails in existence. The spice from the ginger beer balances well against the depth and sweetness of the black currant from the crème de cassis.

½ ounce crème de cassis, such as Giffard
½ ounce lime juice
1½ ounces blanco or reposado tequila
Spicy ginger beer, such as Fever-Tree, to top
Lime wheel, for garnish

☠ Shake crème de cassis, lime juice, and tequila with ice. Strain into a chilled Collins glass full of ice. Top with ginger beer, add straw, and stir gently to integrate. Garnish with the lime wheel and serve with a straw.

NOTE: When buying crème liqueurs, spring for the good stuff. If treated like a vampire—e.g., kept out of sunlight and away from heat sources and garlic—a single bottle will last for years. Cheaper versions often rely on artificial flavoring and may compromise the quality of your finished drink.

SEE YOU IN...

HELL COCKTAIL

There are delicious cocktails, and then there are the drinks you serve your enemies to see how they react. This falls in the latter category and is designed to give hell to your mouth, mind, and stomach. Serve with caution and choose your victims wisely.

1 ounce cognac

1 ounce crème de menthe

Pinch cayenne pepper, for garnish

💀 Shake cognac and crème de menthe with ice. Strain into a chilled rocks glass, and garnish with a pinch of cayenne pepper.

NOT A SMOKING GUN

REVOLVER

This modern classic drinks like a sophisticated coffee Old Fashioned. To take the name a step further, the recipe originally called for Bulleit bourbon, which loads even more meaning in. Like its namesake, it carries quite the punch.

2 ounces bourbon
½ ounce coffee liqueur, such as Borghetti
2 dashes orange bitters
Flamed orange peel, for garnish

☠ Stir bourbon, coffee liqueur, and orange bitters with ice. Strain into a chilled rocks glass over a large cube. Flame the orange peel, and drop the peel into the drink.

MAD MIXOLOGY: Flaming an orange peel is one of the most impressive bar tricks in existence. Cut a disc or wide rectangle of orange peel from a firm orange. Hold the peel gently by its edges, with the pith side of the peel facing the ground. Using a butane lighter or long-stemmed match, heat the white side of the peel. When the colorful side is shiny, hold this side towards the surface of the drink. Move the flame between the peel and the drink and squeeze the peel hard to express the oils through the flame.

LET THE BLOOD FLOW

SANGRIA

With a name that translates to "bloodletting," the ubiquity and popularity of this drink is a bit surprising. In this context, its use in the movie *Climax* as the catalyst for gore and horror seems a bit on the nose.

For your next ritual—er, party—consider batching a pitcher or two. Sangria is incredibly easy to mix and can be jazzed up with seasonal fruit or left as is. You can play with different juices, liquors, and wine varietals to change the flavor, but for experimental rigor, find a base recipe you love and tweak one or two ingredients at a time.

1 (750 ml) bottle dry red wine

¼ cup brandy

1 ounce Simple Syrup (see recipe on page 19)

2 oranges, sliced (or ½ cup orange juice)

½ lemon, sliced

1 green apple, cored and sliced

☠ In a pitcher or punch bowl, stir the wine, brandy, and sugar until no granules remain. Add the sliced fruit. Refrigerate for at least an hour.

MAD MIXOLOGY: To develop new cocktails, most bartenders start with a tried and true classic recipe and change one or two ingredients at a time. At every step, they write down their changes, and when the beverage is perfected, they make extensive notes on the process. Having a notebook or scribbling in the margins of a recipe is a time-honored tradition in the field. Try it here!

TWIRLING HIS MUSTACHE EITHER WAY

SATAN'S WHISKERS

Possibly created for Hollywood starlets during Prohibition as a riff on the Bronx cocktail (see below), this cocktail will have you twirling your own mustache even if you don't have facial hair. The slight differences among the two tipples' names refer to the orange liqueur used, but you would have to ask Beelzebub himself about the base name's origin.

SATAN'S WHISKERS, STRAIGHT

½ ounce gin

½ ounce sweet vermouth

½ ounce dry vermouth

¼ ounce Grand Marnier

½ ounce fresh orange juice

3 dashes orange bitters

Orange peel, for garnish

SATAN'S WHISKERS, CURLED

½ ounce gin

½ ounce sweet vermouth

½ ounce dry vermouth

¼ ounce orange curaçao

½ ounce fresh orange juice

3 dashes orange bitters

Orange peel, for garnish

☠ Shake liquid ingredients with ice. Strain into a chilled coupe glass, and garnish with the orange peel.

VARIATIONS: Ditch the orange liqueur, and bump the gin to 1½ ounces and the orange juice to ¾ ounce for a **Bronx**.

SATAN'S WHISKERS, CURLED
See page 96

RATED R

Surprisingly few horror movie villains drink alcohol on-screen. But if they were to encounter a bartender in their downtime, these are the drinks they might order if given the chance.

HE'S AN AMERICAN BOY...

AMERICANO

There is nothing more American than a horror movie set at a summer camp. Thus, Jason Voorhees from the *Friday the 13th* series gets an Americano. It's the perfect refresher for a summer evening and is low enough proof not to interfere with any murder-y plans later on. Further, since vermouth is bittered with different barks and Campari was colored with beetles up until 2006, the ingredients parallel Vorhees's backstory of growing up as a feral child in the woods.

1½ ounces sweet vermouth
1½ ounces Campari
Chilled soda water, to top
Orange peel, for garnish

💀 Pour sweet vermouth and Campari into a chilled Collins glass filled with ice. Top with soda water, and stir gently to combine. Garnish with the orange peel and serve with a straw.

VARIATIONS: Swap out Campari for Rabarbaro, a rhubarb amaro, to make a **Mezzo E Mezzo**.

BEWARE OF CREEPY NEIGHBORS

FRIGHT NIGHT

Kaley Brodur, beverage director for The Ibis and The Starling, Wilmington, NC

Watching the original or remake of *Fright Night* requires popcorn. Although this could be extended to almost any horror movie, Brodur named this concoction to evoke the flavors of a movie theater. But please, at least listen to your kid if they try to tell you the next-door neighbor is a vampire, especially if their best friend goes missing.

1½ ounces Popcorn-Washed Rum, such as Planteray 5 Year (see recipe)
¾ ounce Cocchi Americano
½ ounce Brown Sugar Simple Syrup (see recipe)
½ ounce lime juice

☠ Shake Popcorn-Washed Rum, Cocchi Americano, Brown Sugar Syrup, and lime juice well with ice. Strain into a chilled coupe glass.

POPCORN-WASHED RUM: Pop one ½ cup serving of popcorn kernels following the instructions. Add 1 teaspoon salt while still hot. Place the popcorn in a heat-proof, sealable vessel such as a Cambro or large mason jar, and pour 1 (750 ml) bottle of rum over top. Let infuse for 12 to 24 hours. Strain into quart containers and freeze overnight. Pour through a coffee filter to strain.

BROWN SUGAR SIMPLE SYRUP: Combine 600 grams brown sugar with 600 grams hot water, and stir until all sugar is dissolved.

THEY'RE BEHIND YOU

IN THE BAR WITH A KNIFE

Joe Witkowski, Dining Room Manager at 34 Restaurant and Bar, New Orleans, LA

If given the chance, Ghostface from the Scream franchise would absolutely kill you in the bar with a knife. Or anywhere. For that reason, if the current mask-wearing murderer saw this cocktail on a menu, we believe they would definitely order it.

The cocktail itself was inspired by the game of Clue and the opportunities for murder mysteries around Halloween. Witkowski designed this cocktail to be a little smoky, a little sweet, and completely dangerous in large quantities. Lock up your knives . . .

1 ½ ounces mezcal, such as El Buho

1 ounce dry vermouth, such as Dolin Blanc

2 barspoons fig preserves

3 drops aromatic bitters, such as Scrappy's

Maraschino cherry, such as Luxardo, for garnish

💀 Shake mezcal, dry vermouth, fig preserves, and bitters well with ice. Strain into a chilled coupe glass, and garnish with the cherry.

GET TO THE CHOPPER!

MANHATTAN

In recent years, one of the best horror-related jokes is that the Hunters from the *Predator* films are the intergalactic equivalent of rich folks on safari. To extend this quip, if given the chance, these Hunters might drink Manhattans, likely made with an expensive bourbon.

Joking aside, the Manhattan has spawned many riffs over its century of popularity because it is both versatile and delicious. Enjoy—and watch out for those tracking lasers.

2 ounces bourbon whiskey

1 ounce sweet vermouth

2 dashes aromatic bitters, such as Angostura

Orange peel and maraschino cherry, for garnish

💀 Mix bourbon, sweet vermouth, and aromatic bitters well with ice. Strain into a chilled cocktail glass, and garnish with the orange and cherry.

VARIATIONS: Substitute Averna for sweet vermouth and rye for bourbon to make a **Black Manhattan**. To make a **Rob Roy**, swap Scotch for bourbon and use just ¾ ounce sweet vermouth. Finally, replace bourbon with rye and use ¾ ounce sweet vermouth for a **Remember the Maine**.

I'D GIVE ANYTHING FOR A DRINK

MARTINI

In the novel version of *The Shining*, Jack Torrance orders a Martini in the bar as the hotel's influence on him strengthens and the spirits gather. In the movie version, he orders a bourbon and is served a Jack Daniels (which is not bourbon). Kubrick's reason for changing the drink has inspired many fan theories.

Martini preferences are one of the most strongly held stances in drinking. Whether it is made shaken or stirred, dry or wet, vodka or gin, orange bitters or none, and garnished with a twist or an olive makes a difference in the resulting drink's flavor. Experiment until you find your perfect combination.

2 ounces gin
¼ to 1 ounce dry vermouth
2 dashes orange bitters (optional)
Lemon twist or olives, for garnish

💀 Stir or shake the spirit, dry vermouth, and optional bitters. Strain into a chilled martini glass, and garnish with your garnish of choice.

NOTE: Jack Daniels is a Tennessee whiskey, not a bourbon. A few differences exist between the two categories: the former is defined on the state level and must be filtered through charcoal. Bourbon is defined on the national level and is not filtered. The delineation is likely due to big brands' lobbying: this distinction allows Jim Beam to market itself as the top-selling bourbon in the world, while Jack Daniels is the number one whiskey.

VARIATIONS: Substitute sweet vermouth for dry, use the orange bitters, and garnish with an orange twist to make a **Martinez**.

GLOOMY GREEN GLOW

MIDORI SOUR

Let's face it, a Midori Sour resembles the aliens' color in *Alien 3*. As a result, this drink is what we think a Xenomorph would drink.

1 ounce melon liqueur, such as Midori
1 ounce vodka
½ ounce lemon juice
½ ounce lime juice
Club soda, to top
Lemon wheel, for garnish

💀 Pour the first four liquid ingredients into a chilled Collins glass filled with ice. Stir gently to combine, add club soda, and stir again briefly. Garnish with the lemon wheel.

GOT MILK?

Milk (Punch)

There is a curious trend in horror movies of menacing figures drinking milk. Although the significance varies from movie to movie, Alex in *A Clockwork Orange*, Ash from *Alien*, Rose in *Get Out*, and Norman Bates from *Psycho* all drink milk on screen.

We've decided that their alcoholic drink of choice might be a Brandy Milk Punch—and not the batched and clarified kind.

2 ounces cognac

1½ ounces whole milk

1 ounce high-proof aged rum

½ ounce Simple Syrup (see recipe on page 19)

Grated nutmeg, for garnish

☠ Shake cognac, milk, rum, and Simple Syrup well with 1 to 2 cups shaved or crushed ice. Pour into chilled rocks glass, and grate fresh nutmeg over top.

FIT FOR A COUNT

NEGRONI

If Count Dracula could drink anything other than blood, he would absolutely enjoy the Negroni. This bitter beverage requires a refined palate and was created more than a century ago by a fellow Count, Camillo Negroni. With Dracula's several centuries as the undead, one (or three) of these could bring a smile to his face. Perhaps the two counts even crossed paths. Or swords.

But reader, beware—the flavor range of sweet vermouths on the market varies from incredibly bitter, like Punt E Mes to balanced, like Dolin Rouge; to unobtrusive, like Martini & Rossi. Likewise, types of gin range from the sweet, floral, and sippable Old Tom to the incredibly herbal London Dry. Experiment with different types to find the perfect combination for you.

1 ounce London Dry gin
1 ounce sweet vermouth
1 ounce Campari
Orange peel, for garnish

💀 Combine all liquid ingredients in a mixing glass. Add ice and stir until chilled, about 15 to 20 seconds. Strain into a rocks glass over one large cube and garnish with the orange peel.

VARIATIONS: Swap prosecco for gin to make a **Negroni Sbagliato**; whiskey to mix a **Boulevardier**; tequila for a **Rosita**; and Jamaican rum for a **Kingston Negroni**. For a less bitter modern build, increase the gin to 1½ ounces and decrease the Campari to ½ ounce. Substitute dry vermouth for the sweet and Suze for the Campari into the modern recipe to make a **White Negroni**.

DON'T MAKE A SOUND

ONE SINGLE TEAR

Christina Mae Henderson, Redroom Cocktail Lounge, Santa Cruz, CA

Named for the scene in *The City of Lost Children* where a single tear sets off a consequential series of events, this cocktail is likewise playful and incredibly complex.

3 mint leaves

1 ounce vodka, such as Barr Hill

1 ounce Hpnotiq

½ ounce lemon juice

3 dashes Life Everlasting Tincture

Soda water, to top

Mint sprig, for garnish

☠ Gently muddle mint leaves in a shaker tin. Add vodka, Hpnotiq, lemon juice, tincture, and ice, and shake well. Strain into a chilled Collins glass and garnish with the mint sprig.

NOTE: Life Everlasting Tincture can be found under its common name or as helichrysum arenarium, a golden yellow flower with a curry-like scent.

END THE SUFFERING

PAINKILLER

For author Paul Sheldon in *Misery*, drugging his captor with painkillers is one way he tries to escape. Annie, his biggest fan and a former nurse, would have drunk a Painkiller if she had mixed them each a cocktail rather than pouring a couple glasses of wine.

2 ounces overproof rum

1½ ounces pineapple juice

¾ ounce fresh orange juice

¾ ounce cream of coconut

Pineapple wedge, maraschino cherry, and grated nutmeg for garnish

☠ Shake rum, juices, and cream of coconut well without ice. Strain into a chilled tiki mug over ice and garnish with the pineapple wedge, cherry, and grated nutmeg.

AGAINST THE LAW

SCOFFLAW

Not all big bads have a criminal history, but Michael Myers sure does. All of his killing sprees in the *Halloween* series occur after he escapes his jail time for killing his older sister, and the police are serially unable to keep him locked up. His flouting the law time and again makes the Scofflaw the perfect choice.

1 ½ ounces rye whiskey

1 ounce dry vermouth

¾ ounce lime juice

½ ounce grenadine

¼ ounce Simple Syrup (see recipe on page 19)

1 dash orange bitters

Orange twist, for garnish

☠ Shake whiskey, vermouth, lime juice, grenadine, and bitters well with ice. Strain into a chilled cocktail glass and garnish with the orange twist.

DON'T FALL ASLEEP

SLEEPYHEAD

As long as you don't sleep, Freddy cannot enter your dreams. But when you are safe from Kreuger, may we recommend a Sleepy Head as a nightcap?

Orange peel or orange slice

4 mint leaves

½ ounce brandy

½ ounce lemon juice

Ginger ale, to top

Mint leaves, for garnish

💀 Muddle orange peel well in a shaker. Muddle mint leaves gently. Add brandy and lemon juice to the shaker and shake well with ice. Strain into a chilled Collins glass filled with ice, and top with ginger ale. Garnish with the mint leaves.

MAD MIXOLOGY: Smashing mint into bits releases chlorophyll from the leaves in addition to the mint oil. Chlorophyll is bitter and earthy, so to minimize its introduction, use a muddler to lightly tap the leaves just until you can smell the mint.

BLESSED BE THE MAY QUEEN

SOUTHSIDE

Light and refreshing, this drink is perfect around the summer solstice. But do not be fooled: the Southside comes with a kick, and too many of them will have you seeing visions in the fire or trusting strangers a little too readily. If the Hårga in *Midsommar* drank anything outside their psychedelic tea, they might have reached for this drink.

6 to 8 mint leaves
2 ounces gin
¾ ounce lime juice
¾ ounce Simple Syrup (see recipe on page 19)
Mint leaf, for garnish

☠ Gently muddle (see note on muddling on page 124) mint leaves in a shaker. Add gin, lime juice, and Simple Syrup, and shake with ice. Strain into a chilled coupe glass, and garnish with the mint leaf.

VARIATIONS: Substitute lemon juice for lime to make a **Gin Smash**. Substitute bourbon for gin and lemon juice for lime to make a **Whiskey Smash**. Switch rum for gin, use a Collins glass, and top with soda water to make a **Mojito**. Ditch the mint, substitute lemon juice for lime, and top with soda in a Collins glass to make a **Tom Collins**.

GIN SMASH
See page 127

IN THE END, THE PAST ALWAYS CATCHES UP TO YOU

SUMMERTIME

At the end of a long summer, all anyone wants is a simple drink to help beat the heat. As a result, the Summertime would be the cocktail of choice for Ben Willis and basically anyone else from the *I Know What You Did Last Summer* franchise. Modified from the recipe in *The Savoy Cocktail Book*, this cocktail is extremely similar to a Tom Collins.

1½ ounces gin
½ ounce Simple Syrup (see recipe on page 19)
½ ounce lemon juice
Soda water, to top

☠ Shake gin, Simple Syrup, and lemon juice well with ice. Strain into a double rocks glass filled with ice, then top with soda water.

MAD MIXOLOGY: If you want to make the original recipe, substitute the Simple Syrup with sirop de citron. This can either be bought as Monin Lemon Syrup, which is a bit sweeter than the traditional sirop or by making it at home. To make it at home, wash and thinly slice about a pound of lemons and place in a glass jar. Add 2 cups sugar and seal. For the next 48 to 72 hours, roll the jar on the counter 3 to 4 times a day. After three days, move the lemon and sugar mixture to a pan and simmer until all the sugar is dissolved. Strain well, and add water to taste. Store in a clean glass jar. Mixture should keep refrigerated for 2 to 3 weeks.

CREATURE FEATURE

Monsters are deeply rooted in spooky folklore stories, and many drinks and their ingredients have their roots in pre-pharmaceutical medicine. These cocktails made their way into this book through their associations with aspects of specific creatures' mythologies.

Before the rise of most modern pharmaceuticals in the early 1900s, treatments for different ailments were largely herbal. Many of the alcohol-based ingredients now used primarily behind bars were at one time prescribed by doctors. Angostura bitters were developed as a cure-all for soldiers; Fernet-Branca was originally marketed as a cure for menstrual cramps; and many of the multitude of other bitters decommissioned by the advent of the FDA claimed to cure just about everything.

But the history of medicinal alcohol is much more expansive than only a few products. Whiskey could be purchased legally during Prohibition—as long as you had a prescription. Distilled alcohol was used for centuries as an anesthetic. In the heyday of the British navy, sailors fought scurvy by mixing their citrus rations with their liquor rations. The lore runs deep

COMMUNE WITH SPIRITS

ALMAS PERDIDAS

Chris Mansury, Cantina Pedregal del Norte, Folsom, CA

Lose yourself in dreams or drinks, and you might just find that you've become one of the lost souls.

1 ½ ounces sotol, such as La Escondida
1 ounce Watermelon Cordial (see recipe)
¾ ounce lime juice
1 barspoon Ancho Chile Tincture (see recipe)
1 barspoon Bruto Americano
Bat gummies, for garnish

💀 Shake sotol, Watermelon Cordial, lime juice, Ancho Chile Tincture, and Bruto Americano well with ice. Strain into a saline-rinsed glass and garnish with the gummies.

WATERMELON CORDIAL: Combine equal parts watermelon juice and Simple Syrup (see recipe on page 19).

ANCHO CHILE TINCTURE: Add 3 dried ancho chiles to ¾ cup 100-proof vodka. Let steep for three days, then take out the chiles.

CREATURE FEATURE   137

EVERY ONCE IN A WHILE

BLUE MOON

In most mythologies, werewolves can only shift into their wolf form during the full moon. Although this isn't the case for all stories of the wolfmen, stories where they're in control regardless of what's in the sky are as rare as the blue moon.

2 ounces gin

¾ ounce lemon juice

½ ounce crème de violette

Lemon twist, for garnish

☠ Shake gin, lemon juice, and crème de violette well with ice. Strain into a chilled cocktail glass and garnish with the lemon twist.

VARIATIONS: For an **Aviation**, use only ¼ ounce crème de violette and add ½ ounce maraschino liqueur. Ditch the lemon twist and garnish with the maraschino cherry.

AVIATION
See page 138

GO SUCK A GOAT

CHUPACABRA

Mark Schettler, executive director of Shift Change and New Orleans bartender

Native to the Americas, the chupacabra is a vampiric cryptid that feeds on livestock, especially goats. Although some veterinarians believe that sightings of this cryptid may have been coyotes with extreme mange or a weird breed of dog, warnings to watch out for this monster persist.

¾ ounce blanco tequila

¾ ounce joven mezcal

¾ ounce Suze

¾ ounce blanco Basque Spanish vermouth, such as Tximista

Grapefruit peel ribbon or swath, for garnish

💀 Stir tequila, mezcal, Suze, and vermouth well with ice. Strain into a chilled rocks glass over a large cube and garnish with the grapefruit peel.

CREATURE FEATURE

THERE BE DRAGONS

EMERALD GIMLET

If one thing is certain in tabletop gaming, it is that a dragon's lair always has a stash of treasure. In some stories, dragons can shapeshift into human form. There, they would surround themselves in lavish jewel-tone furnishings . . . and equally beautiful drinks.

2 ounces gin
¾ ounce Simple Syrup (see recipe on page 19)
¾ ounce lime juice
3 to 4 drops green food coloring
Lime wheel, for garnish

💀 Shake gin, Simple Syrup, lime juice, and food coloring well with ice. Strain into a chilled coupe glass, and garnish with the lime wheel.

VARIATIONS: Substitute rum for gin to make a classic **Daiquiri**. Substitute vodka to make a **Vodka Gimlet**.

VODKA GIMLET

See page 144

BEWARE BOX #5

FRENCH 75

As a villain of culture and refined taste, Erik—the famed phantom of *The Phantom of the Opera*—would both drink and serve the French 75. The musical genius haunted the theater, but with the booze leftover from cast parties and champagne from opening night, he'd likely be able to make this cocktail with what was lying around.

1 ounce gin

½ ounce Simple Syrup (see recipe on page 19)

½ ounce lemon juice

Champagne, to top

Lemon twist, for garnish

💀 Shake gin, Simple Syrup, and lemon juice well with ice. Strain into a chilled champagne flute and top with champagne. Garnish with the lemon twist.

VARIATIONS: Substitute bourbon for gin to mix a **French 95**, brandy for a **King's Peg**, and tequila for a **Mexican 75**.

WHEN THE MOON HITS YOUR EYES

MOONLIGHT

Some historians believe that the idea of vampirism is at least partially based on word-of-mouth accounts from patients with rabies. Most stories outside of the *Twilight* series include biting, blood, and sensitivity to light. As a result, these nightwalkers conduct all their outdoor business by moonlight.

1½ ounces London Dry gin
1¼ ounces grapefruit juice
1 ounce sauvignon blanc
½ ounce kirschwasser
Lime twist, to garnish

☠ Shake gin, grapefruit juice, sauvignon blanc, and kirschwasser well with ice. Strain into a chilled cocktail glass, and garnish with the lime twist.

BANE AND CURE

SILVER BULLET

Silver has long been believed to be an effective weapon against monsters because of its purity. In werewolf lore specifically, beheading, silver, fire, and wolfsbane are typically noted as the main ways to kill or injure the creature. For modern tales, their death often comes at the business end of a silver bullet or knife.

As a drink, the Silver Bullet is complex and refreshing. Kümmel, a Dutch herbal liqueur, teases out the spice flavors in the gin, and the lemon cuts through the sweetness to provide a drink fit for the full moon. Although the original recipe doesn't call for Simple Syrup, the addition helps to balance the recipe to more modern tastes.

½ ounce kümmel, such as Combier

¼ ounce Simple Syrup (see recipe on page 19)

¾ ounce lemon juice

2 ounces London Dry gin

Lemon zest, for garnish

💀 Combine liquid ingredients in a cocktail shaker. Add ice and shake until chilled through, about 15 to 20 seconds. Strain into a chilled coupe or Nick and Nora glass, and garnish with the lemon zest.

RATTLESNAKES, BASILISKS, AND SEA SERPENTS, OH MY!

SNAKEBITE

Snakes are part of most cultures' myths, either as monsters or as symbols of forbidden knowledge. Their bite and their gaze are usually portrayed as their most dangerous—if not outright deadly—weapons, and their presence is usually a harbinger of bad things to come.

This drink is one of only a few classic beer cocktails, but it is imminently sippable. Watch out for its bite.

5 to 6 ounces hard cider

5 to 6 ounces lager

☠ Fill a chilled pint glass halfway with hard cider, and fill the rest with lager.

VARIATIONS: Swap in lemonade for cider and pale ale for lager to make a **Shandy**; substitute lemonade for cider and German beer for lager for a **Radler**.

SHANDY
See page 156

RADLER
See page 156

YOU BE THE JUDGE

STINGER

Some bugs are a sign of a dirty environment, but others clean with their presence. They skitter and bite and swarm and move in unsettling ways. But the bugs that sting are often the scariest, especially if they are multitude.

2 ounces brandy

¾ ounce white crème de menthe

☠ Shake brandy and crème de menthe well with ice and strain into a chilled cocktail glass.

VARIATIONS: Substitute light rum for brandy to mix a **Picador**, or swap in vodka for a **White Spider**. Add two dashes aromatic bitters, such as Angostura, and garnish with a lemon peel for a **Brant**.

CREATURE FEATURE

PICADOR
See page 161

BRANT
See page 161

LIFE'S FULL OF TOUGH CHOICES

URSULA

Kate Gerwin, owner of Happy Accidents in Albuquerque, NM

As one of the more interesting Disney villains, Ursula either portrayed as an evil sea hag or as a woman who wanted her legally binding contract enforced. Though stealing someone's voice is never cool, this cocktail is. The combination of sour yogurt soda, white chocolate, and ube gives this purple drink a rich, nutty, and slightly floral character.

2 ounces vodka

½ ounce white chocolate syrup, such as Monin

1 drop ube extract, such as Butterfly Brand

2 dashes lavender bitters

Japanese yogurt soda such as Calpico, to top

☠ Shake vodka, white chocolate syrup, ube extract, and lavender bitters well with ice. Strain into a brandy snifter over crushed ice and top with the yogurt soda.

DANGER AHEAD

WHITE LADY

Stories of encounters with the Lady in White—also called the Woman in White or La Llorona—crop up repeatedly across cultures. Typically, the mythologies center around lost love, with the ghost in question often causing car accidents by appearing suddenly in the road. Though the specifics of each encounter differ, the ghost is usually wearing white and appears to be weeping.

Egg white

2 ounces gin

¾ ounce lemon juice

½ ounce orange liqueur

¼ ounce Simple Syrup (see recipe on page 19)

☠ Shake egg white, gin, lemon juice, orange liqueur, and Simple Syrup well without ice. Add ice, shake well again, and strain into a chilled coupe glass.

CREATURE FEATURE 169

BRAAAAAINS

ZOMBIE

Few cocktails are directly named for mythical creatures. The Zombie is an exception. The name derives from the cocktail's strength: even modern tiki bars limit patrons to two before they are cut off. Beware its bite, as it may turn you into a zombie too.

1½ ounces Jamaican rum
1½ ounces Puerto Rican rum
1 ounce overproof rum
¾ ounce lime juice
½ ounce Don's Mix (see recipe)
½ ounce Velvet Falernum

¼ ounce grenadine
2 dashes absinthe
1 dash aromatic bitters, such as Angostura
Mint sprig, for garnish

Shake all liquid ingredients well with ice. Strain into a chilled tiki mug filled with ice and garnish with the mint sprig.

NOTE: Don the Beachcomber was notoriously tight-lipped about the syrups and premixed ingredients that went into his cocktails. This secrecy was so intense that recreating these flavors after his death took many hours of investigation, experimenting, taste testing, and interviews with former employees.

DON'S MIX: Combine 1½ cups grapefruit juice with ¾ cup cinnamon syrup. To make cinnamon syrup, combine 1 cup sugar with one cup hot water. Mix until sugar has dissolved, and add 1 to 2 cinnamon sticks. Cover and let sit overnight. Strain, and store in an airtight container in the refrigerator.

"BOO"ZE-FREE DRINKS

In the modern bar scene, quite a few bartenders and guests don't actually drink. Most people recognize that offering spirit-free cocktails is good hospitality. This chapter provides some non-alcoholic options for those who choose not to imbibe for whatever reason.

Beware of calling these sips "mocktails." The drinks that follow are as complex as any alcoholic cocktail and do not try to imitate alcoholic beverages. Instead, they're crafted not to mimic the taste of alcohol but to stand strong on their own flavor profiles.

PULPY GOODNESS

BLOOD ORANGE COOLER

As far as juices go, blood oranges are aptly named. This refresher showcases the vibrant color of this citrus and adds in a few complementary flavors to make it shine.

2 ounces blood orange juice

1 ounce grenadine

3 drops vanilla extract

2 dashes aromatic bitters, such as Angostura

Blood orange wheel and rosemary sprig, for garnish

☠ Shake blood orange juice, grenadine, vanilla extract, and aromatic bitters well with ice. Strain into a chilled coupe glass and garnish with the blood orange wheel and rosemary sprig.

MAD MIXOLOGY: If you're trying to avoid alcohol entirely, use glycerin-based bitters such as Fee Brothers. Many common brands of bitters including Angostura and Peychaud's are made with non-potable alcohol. Just as using bitters doesn't make a drink bitter, adding a few dashes will only add trace amounts of alcohol.

JUST KEEP SWIMMING

FROM THE DEPTHS

Although the ocean covers 71 percent of the Earth's surface, what lies beneath the waves is largely a mystery. Writers and sailors have told stories of monsters like giant sea squids, leviathans, and colossal prehistoric sharks since humans began sailing the seas. But what awaits adventurous souls under the surface—much less seven miles down in the Mariana Trench—is anyone's guess.

3 to 5 mint leaves

1½ ounces blue raspberry syrup

1½ ounces lemon juice

1 ounce water

Gummy shark, for garnish

💀 Muddle the mint leaves in a chilled brandy snifter and fill with ice. Shake blue raspberry syrup, lemon juice, and water well with ice. Strain into the snifter and garnish with the gummy shark.

JUST MULL IT OVER

Mulled Cider

Nothing staves off the cold in winter quite like mulled cider. Warming spices accentuate the tartness and sweetness of the cider, and its easy recipe makes it a great addition to any winter night. This recipe yields about 16 cups.

- 1 gallon apple cider
- 4 cinnamon sticks
- 1½ teaspoons whole allspice
- 1 teaspoon whole cloves
- 1 orange, peeled and sliced
- Orange wheel, for garnish

☠ In a saucepan or slow cooker, heat the cider with the spices and orange slices. Cover and simmer for about 45 minutes, or until fragrant. To serve, ladle 6 to 8 ounces into preheated mugs using the trick on page 210. Garnish with the orange wheel.

VARIATIONS: To make a boozy version, add 1 cup rum. Substitute 1 (750 ml) bottle of dry red wine for 12 cups apple cider, add 2 star anise pods, and the juice of one orange to make **Mulled Wine**.

MULLED WINE
See page 179

THEY'RE WAITING

NIGHTMARE TONIC

Whether this potion will inspire your deepest nightmares or protect your dreaming sleep may depend on the maker's intention. Or perhaps your nighttime visions were fated before today even began . . .

2 blackberries

3 ounces pomegranate juice

1 ounce unsweetened tart cherry juice

1 ounce maple syrup

2 drops black food coloring

Lemon or lime soda water, to top

2 maraschino cherries on a pick and edible glitter, for garnish

☠ Muddle blackberries well in a shaker. Add pomegranate juice, cherry juice, maple syrup, and food coloring and shake well with ice. Strain into a chilled Collins glass and fill with ice. Top with soda water, and garnish with the cherries and edible glitter.

IT'S MAGICAL

PUMPKIN JUICE

At a favorite wizarding academy and the associated theme park, students take field trips to the local town, where they are able to sample magical delights. Pumpkin Juice is a lovely fall treat for all visitors, bringing together much-beloved pumpkin spice syrup, apple cider, and pumpkin puree.

2 liters apple cider

1 cup pumpkin puree

½ cup brown sugar

1 cup Pumpkin Spice Simple Syrup (see recipe)

1 teaspoon vanilla extract

☠ Combine cider, pumpkin puree, brown sugar, Pumpkin Spice Simple Syrup, and vanilla extract in a blender. Blend well to combine, pour into chilled glasses, and serve with a straw.

PUMPKIN SPICE SIMPLE SYRUP: Combine 1 cup sugar with 1 cup hot water. Stir until sugar is dissolved, and add 4 to 5 cinnamon sticks, ½ teaspoon nutmeg, ½ teaspoon ground ginger, and ½ teaspoon ground cloves. Stir to combine. Let the cinnamon sticks sit in the syrup for 2 to 4 hours, and remove. Store in an airtight glass jar in the refrigerator.

SEEING STARS

RITUAL VISIONS

Veronica Flores, bar lead at Marlow in Austin, TX

For a cocktail that's equal parts mystical and richly flavorful with just a hint of spice, check out Flores's dreamy tipple. The Gochujang Caramel takes a little effort, but darling, the most effective rituals always do.

1½ ounces non-alcoholic whiskey, such as Ritual Non-Alcoholic Whiskey Alternative

1½ ounces apple cider

¾ ounce Gochujang Caramel (see recipe)

¼ ounce lemon juice

3 drops Saline Solution (see recipe)

3 drops Citric Acid Solution (see recipe)

Korean chile threads, for garnish

☠ Shake all liquid ingredients well with ice. Strain into a chilled wineglass full of ice and garnish with the chile threads.

GOCHUJANG CARAMEL: Add one cup sugar to a large pot over medium heat and whisk for 45 seconds to begin the caramelization. Add in 1 (13.5 ounce) can of coconut milk, 2 heaping tablespoons gochujang paste, ¼ teaspoon salt, and 1 teaspoon cinnamon, whisking continuously to combine. Turn heat to low and let simmer for 15 minutes. It should thicken up a bit, but do not let it go much longer. Remove from heat and allow to cool before using. Store in an airtight container with a lid and refrigerate.

SALINE SOLUTION: By weight, combine 20 grams salt with 80 grams hot water. Stir until all salt is dissolved.

CITRIC ACID SOLUTION: Combine 2 teaspoons of citric acid with ½ cup hot water. Stir until all citric acid is dissolved.

THE BEATING OF HIS HIDEOUS HEART

TELLTALE HEART

It's a tale as old as time: an unreliable narrator kills a man, buries the man's heart beneath his floorboards, and is driven mad by the sound of it beating. In this drink, the muddled strawberry is hidden beneath ice, and only by drinking can you free it.

2 to 3 small strawberries or 1 large strawberry

2 ounces lemon juice

½ ounce Simple Syrup (see recipe on page 19)

1 ounce pomegranate juice

1 ounce water

1 dash orange bitters

Blood orange wheel, for garnish

💀 In a chilled double rocks glass, muddle the strawberries and fill with ice. Shake lemon juice, Simple Syrup, pomegranate juice, water, and orange bitters well with ice. Strain into the glass and garnish with the blood orange wheel.

WINTER CAMPFIRE TALES

In the days before electric lights, telling ghost stories during the depths of winter was a well-known tradition to pass the darkest nights. Even one of the most famous Christmas stories, Charles Dickens's *A Christmas Carol*, revolves around a haunting.

THE HOLY TRINITY

Café Brulot

During the colder months, alcohol, coffee, and fire are often used to warm up after a hard day's work. Having the patience and fortitude to combine all three into this beverage makes the outcome that much more deliciously refreshing.

- ¾ cup brandy
- 8 whole cloves
- 2 tablespoons sugar or 6 sugar cubes
- 2 cinnamon sticks, broken
- 2 large orange twists
- Lemon twist
- 4 cups hot coffee

💀 Place all of ingredients except the coffee in a chafing dish. Heat gradually, stirring gently with a metal ladle. Set aflame and let burn for about 1 minute. Slowly add coffee. Ladle into small preheated mugs using the trick on page 210, leaving the spices behind.

VARIATIONS: Extend burning period to approximately 2 minutes before adding coffee for a **Café Diable**.

WARNING: Working with a combination of fire and alcohol is dangerous. Do not use a plastic ladle or dish, and do not serve in plastic cups. Exercise extreme caution while the brandy is ablaze, and do not add the coffee until the flames have died down.

FIT FOR A KING

CAFÉ ROYALE

Sometimes a cup of slightly sweet coffee warms you to your bones and makes you feel like royalty. During the winter, the sensation is doubly sweet.

4 to 6 ounces hot coffee

1½ ounces brandy

1 sugar cube

☠ Pour coffee into a warmed mug (see trick on page 210). In a metal spoon or ladle over the coffee, combine the brandy and sugar cube. Set the brandy on fire, and once the fire dies down, pour the mixture into the coffee.

WARNING: Working with a combination of fire and alcohol is dangerous. Do not serve in a plastic mug or use a plastic ladle, and exercise extreme caution around flames.

196 SPOOKY COCKTAILS

FOR WINTERTIME ICED COFFEE DRINKERS

CARAJILLO

Although the exact recipe for the Carajillo varies by country, it is just the ticket for anyone who wants a cold coffee drink even in winter.

1½ ounces espresso or double-strength coffee

1½ ounces Licor 43

2 to 3 coffee beans, for garnish

☠ Shake espresso and Licor 43 well with ice. Strain into a chilled coupe glass and garnish with the coffee beans.

VARIATIONS: Substitute vodka for the Licor 43 and add ½ ounce espresso liqueur to make an **Espresso Martini**.

ESPRESSO MARTINI
See page 199

CAFÉ DIABLE
See page 195

LINK BY LINK

CHARLES DICKENS'S PUNCH

Legendary ghost story author Charles Dickens was also well-known for his love of punch, especially flaming punch. In *A Christmas Carol*, the Ghost of Christmas Present is described as appearing surrounded by steaming bowls of it. But communal drinks, especially flaming ones, were falling out of style in favor of single serving cocktails during the writer's lifetime. Despite the decreased popularity, many of the recipes, including Dickens's own, have survived to the present and are still lovely for winter nights.

¾ cup Demerara sugar

2 cups Jamaican rum

1¼ cups cognac

5 cups black tea or hot water

Peels of 3 lemons

Juice of 3 lemons

Lemon and orange wheels, freshly grated nutmeg, for garnish

💀 Peel the lemons so that no pith remains on the peels. Combine peels and sugar in a heatproof punch bowl. Stir together with a wooden spoon, pressing the peels into the sugar to release the oils. Let sit for 30 minutes. Stir again, and then add rum and cognac. Scoop some of the mixture with a stainless steel spoon, and light on fire with a match. Carefully add the flaming spoonful back to the bowl. Let burn for 2 to 3 minutes, then douse by covering with a heatproof tray or lid. Remove the lemon peels and add the hot tea or water. Garnish with the lemon and orange wheels and serve in teacups or mugs.

I wear the chain I forged in life.
—Jacob Marley, *A Christmas Carol*

CREAMY AND COMFORTING

EGGNOG

With a glass of eggnog in hand, it's difficult to feel anything but joyful during the darkest time of year. This rich, spicy concoction hides quite the kick, so beware drinking too much on days where there is much to do.

12 yolks from large eggs

2 cups sugar

1 teaspoon nutmeg, plus more for garnish

2 cups half-and-half

2 cups heavy cream

2 cups whole milk

1 cup rum

1 cup brandy

1 cup bourbon

💀 Separate the eggs, and set aside the whites. Beat the yolks with sugar and nutmeg until the mixture lightens in color and falls off the whisk in a ribbon. Combine half-and-half, cream, milk, rum, brandy, and bourbon in another bowl. Gradually add the mixture while beating the dairy and alcohol constantly. If you wish, move to large sterilized glass jars and store in the fridge for two weeks to two months; this recipe improves with age. Serve in a chilled glass topped with an additional sprinkle of nutmeg.

NOTE: Aging alcoholic beverages may sound scary, but it's a practice older than refrigeration or commercially available ice.

WINTER CAMPFIRE TALES

JACK FROST'S BITE

FROSTBITE

This concoction hails from the depths of sweet, creamy dive bar cocktail history. Don't be fooled by its richness: the icy blue color and sugary ingredients hide a decent amount of alcohol.

1½ ounces tequila

½ ounce white crème de cacao

½ ounce blue curaçao

½ ounce heavy cream

Maraschino cherry, for garnish

💀 Shake tequila, crème de cacao, curaçao, and heavy cream well with ice. Strain into a rocks glass full of ice, and garnish with the maraschino cherry.

YOU CAN TAKE IT HOT TO GO

HOT BUTTERED RUM

When it is cold and dark, a little bit of butter goes a long way in keeping you warm inside and reviving your spirit from a long walk. Keep the spirits flowing with a single-serving mug of hot buttered rum, but drink up quickly—it has "hot" in the name for a reason.

2 teaspoons brown sugar

1 tablespoon unsalted butter

¼ teaspoon vanilla extract

1 shake cinnamon

1 shake nutmeg

1 shake allspice

4 ounces hot water

2 ounces rum

Cinnamon stick, for garnish

💀 Heat a mug using the trick on page 210. In the mug, muddle the sugar, butter, vanilla, cinnamon, nutmeg, and allspice well. Add rum and hot water, and stir to combine. Garnish with the cinnamon stick.

COZY COMFORT

Hot Toddy

On a cold winter's night, nothing is quite as relaxing as sipping a Hot Toddy. Although it was originally a folk medicine recipe (honey or sourgum to coat a sore throat, pain-numbing alcohol, and hot water or tea to soothe on the way down), the citrus was likely a modern addition as lemons became more widely available. The base spirit varies regionally but defaults to what liquor would have been available in the area more than a century ago. If you aren't a fan of bourbon, swap it out for brandy or rum.

2 ounces bourbon

½ ounce Honey Syrup (see recipe on page 74)

½ ounce lemon juice

Hot water or hot tea, for topping

Cinnamon stick, for garnish

☠ Fill a wide-mouthed mug with hot water to warm. Discard water, and add Honey Syrup, lemon juice, and bourbon. Fill with hot water, and stir to combine. Garnish with the cinnamon stick.

VARIATION: Substitute Scotch for bourbon; use 1 ounce hot tea or water to dissolve 1 teaspoon of Demerara sugar; and add in a piece of lemon zest to make a **Whiskey Skin**.

SNOW DAY SIPPING

IRISH COFFEE

The story goes that Irish Coffee was invented at the Foynes Flying Boat Terminal in Ireland to soothe a plane full of travelers whose international flight had been forced to turn around due to bad weather. After more than 80 years, its ability to brighten spirits even on the worst days remains unmatched.

1½ ounces Irish whiskey
2 teaspoons packed light brown sugar
5 to 6 ounces coffee
Whipped cream and chocolate shavings, for topping

💀 Fill a wide-mouthed mug with hot water to warm while the coffee brews. Dump the water, and add the sugar and whiskey to the mug along with a splash of coffee. Stir until sugar is dissolved. Fill with coffee, leaving about an inch of room. Top with whipped cream and chocolate shavings.

AUTUMN AESTHETICS

PUMPKIN SPICE AND EVERYTHING NICE

Colleen Hughes, beverage director, Tonidandel Brown Restaurant Group, Charlotte, NC

2 ounces spiced rum, such as Carolina's
½ ounce Jack-O'-Lantern Syrup (see recipe)
1 ounce chickory coffee, such as Café du Monde, to float
Vanilla whipped cream and Pumpkin Spice Mix (see recipe), for garnish

💀 Pour rum and Jack-O'-Lantern Syrup into a heated tea cup (see trick on page 210). Float coffee, and top with vanilla whipped cream. Dust with pumpkin spice to garnish.

JACK-O'-LANTERN SYRUP: Remove seeds from a whole pumpkin and roast on a baking sheet for about 30 minutes at 400 degrees. Remove skins, and chop into one-inch cubes, and measure out 3½ cups to use in the syrup. Toast 15 whole cloves, ¼ teaspoon cinnamon, a pinch of freshly grated nutmeg, and a pinch of allspice until fragrant. In a separate pot, bring 2 cups water, 1 tablespoon sorghum molasses, 1 cup granulated sugar, and 1 cup brown sugar to a boil. Reduce to a simmer, add in pumpkin and spices, and let cook uncovered for 30 to 35 minutes. Puree with an immersion blender.

PUMPKIN SPICE MIX: Combine ½ cup sugar, ¼ teaspoon ground cinnamon, ¼ teaspoon grated nutmeg, and 2 pinches edible gold glitter.

DRINK AND SING

WASSAIL

Drinking and singing to ward off spirits during the darkest time of the year? Count me in!

2 gallons apple cider

1½ cups bourbon

¾ cup cranberry juice

¾ cup light brown sugar

10 whole cloves

8 whole peppercorns

5 whole allspice berries

½ inch fresh ginger, peeled and sliced thin

3 cinnamon sticks

Cinnamon sticks and freshly grated nutmeg, for garnish

💀 Tie cloves, peppercorns, allspice berries, ginger, and cinnamon sticks in a cheesecloth bundle. Combine cider, cranberry juice, bourbon, brown sugar, and spice bundle in a large pot over high heat. Bring to a boil, reduce heat to low, and simmer for 30 minutes. Warm mugs using the trick on page 210, and ladle mixture into the mugs, garnishing each with a cinnamon stick and freshly grated nutmeg.

CONVERSION TABLE

Weights

1 oz. = 28 grams
2 oz. = 57 grams
4 oz. (¼ lb.) = 113 grams
8 oz. (½ lb.) = 227 grams
16 oz. (1 lb.) = 454 grams

Volume Measures

⅛ teaspoon = 0.6 ml
¼ teaspoon = 1.23 ml
½ teaspoon = 2.5 ml
1 teaspoon = 5 ml
1 tablespoon (3 teaspoons) = ½ fluid oz. = 15 ml
2 tablespoons = 1 fluid oz. = 29.5 ml
¼ cup (4 tablespoons) = 2 fluid oz. = 59 ml
⅓ cup (5⅓ tablespoons) = 2.7 fluid oz. = 80 ml
½ cup (8 tablespoons) = 4 fluid oz. = 120 ml
⅔ cup (10⅔ tablespoons) = 5.4 fluid oz. = 160 ml
¾ cup (12 tablespoons) = 6 fluid oz. = 180 ml
1 cup (16 tablespoons) = 8 fluid oz. = 240 ml

Temperature Equivalents

°F	°C	Gas Mark
225	110	¼
250	130	½
275	140	1
300	150	2
325	170	3
350	180	4
375	190	5
400	200	6
425	220	7
450	230	8
475	240	9
500	250	10

Length Measures

1/16 inch = 1.6 mm
⅛ inch = 3 mm
¼ inch = 6.35 mm
½ inch = 1.25 cm
¾ inch = 2 cm
1 inch = 2.5 cm

INDEX

A

absinthe
  Arsenic and Old Lace, 20
  Chrysanthemum, 26
  Corpse Reviver No. 2, 83
  Death in the Afternoon, 84
  Monkey Gland, 46
  Sazerac, 70
  Zombie, 170
activated charcoal, 13
Agave Syrup
  (Midnight) Margaritas, 43
Alabazam, 19
allspice
  Mulled Cider, 179
  Wassail, 217
Almas Perdidas, 137
almond bitters
  Virgin's Prayer, 58
Americano, 103
Ancho Chile Tincture
  Almas Perdidas, 137
  recipe, 137
apple brandy
  Horror Hotel, 34
apple cider
  Mulled Cider, 179
  Pumpkin Juice, 185
  Ritual Visions, 186
  Wassail, 217
applejack
  The Secret Cocktail, 53
apples
  Sangria, 95
apricot liqueur
  Horror Hotel, 34
Armagnac
  Corpse Reviver No. 1, 80
aromatic bitters
  Alabazam, 19
  In the Bar with a Knife, 107
  Blood Orange Cooler, 175
  Horses' Neck, 39
  Manhattan, 108
  Suburban, 54

Suffering Bastard, 57
Vieux Carré, 73
Zombie, 170
Arsenic and Old Lace, 20

B

beer
  Snakebite, 156
Bénédictine
  Chrysanthemum, 26
  Vieux Carré, 73
black food coloring, 13
blackberries
  Nightmare Tonic, 182
Blood Orange Cooler, 175
Bloody Mary, 23
Blue Devil, 79
Blue Moon, 138
bourbon
  Chatham Artillery Punch, 65
  Eggnog, 205
  Gold Rush, 74
  Horses' Neck, 39
  Hot Toddy, 210
  Manhattan, 108
  Revolver, 92
  Wassail, 217
brandy
  Café Brulot, 195
  Café Royale, 196
  Eggnog, 205
  Filmograph, 30
  Fog Cutter, 33
  Sangria, 95
  Sleepyhead, 124
  Stinger, 161
  Suffering Bastard, 57
brandy, apple
  Horror Hotel, 34
brandy, cherry
  Virgin's Prayer, 58
Brown Sugar Simple Syrup
  Fright Night, 104
  recipe, 104
Bruto Americano

Almas Perdidas, 137

C

Café Brulot, 195
Café Royale, 196
Calvados
  Corpse Reviver No. 1, 80
Campari
  Americano, 103
  Negroni, 116
Candied Lemon Wheels, 30
Carajillo, 199
celery
  Bloody Mary, 23
champagne
  Chatham Artillery Punch, 65
  Death in the Afternoon, 84
  French 75, 149
charcoal, activated, 13
Charles Dickens's Punch, 202
Chartreuse, Green
  Last Word, 40
Chatham Artillery Punch, 65
cherry brandy
  Virgin's Prayer, 58
cherry juice
  Nightmare Tonic, 182
chicory coffee
  Pumpkin Spice and Everything
    Nice, 214
chocolate syrup, white
  Ursula, 166
Chrysanthemum, 26
Chupacabra, 143
cider, apple
  Mulled Cider, 179
  Pumpkin Juice, 185
  Ritual Visions, 186
  Wassail, 217
cider, hard
  Snakebite, 156
Cinnamon Agave Syrup
  Obsidian Butterfly, 49
  recipe, 49
cinnamon sticks

Café Brulot, 195
  Wassail, 217
cinnamon syrup
  Don's Mix, 170
  Zombie, 170
Citric Acid Solution
  Ritual Visions, 186
cloves
  Café Brulot, 195
  Mulled Cider, 179
  Wassail, 217
Cocchi Americano Bianco
  Corpse Reviver No. 2, 83
  Fright Night, 104
coconut milk
  Gochujang Caramel, 186
  Ritual Visions, 186
coffee
  Café Brulot, 195
  Café Royale, 196
  Carajillo, 199
  Irish Coffee, 213
  Pumpkin Spice and Everything
    Nice, 214
coffee beans
  Carajillo, 199
coffee liqueur
  Revolver, 92
cognac
  Alabazam, 19
  Charles Dickens's Punch, 202
  Chatham Artillery Punch, 65
  Hell Cocktail, 91
  Milk (Punch), 115
  Vieux Carré, 73
Cointreau
  Alabazam, 19
  Corpse Reviver No. 2, 83
  (Midnight) Margaritas, 43
conversion table, 218
copper mugs, 13
Corpse Reviver No. 1, 80
Corpse Reviver No. 2, 83
cranberry juice
  Wassail, 217

cream, heavy
  Eggnog, 205
  Frostbite, 206
  Ramos Gin Fizz, 69
cream of coconut
  Painkiller, 120
crème de cacao, white
  Frostbite, 206
crème de cassis
  El Diablo, 88
crème de menthe
  Hell Cocktail, 91
crème de menthe, white
  Stinger, 161
crème de violette
  Arsenic and Old Lace, 20
  Blue Moon, 138
curaçao, blue
  Frostbite, 206
curaçao, orange
  Satan's Whiskers, 96
Cynar
  Horror Hotel, 34

D
Dark 'n' Stormy
  Chrysanthemum, 29
Death in the Afternoon, 84
Demerara Syrup
  recipe, 54
  Suburban, 54
  Suffering Bastard, 57
Devil's Cocktail, 87
Don's Mix
  recipe, 170
  Zombie, 170
dry ice, 13

E
Eggnog, 205
eggs/egg whites
  Eggnog, 205
  Ramos Gin Fizz, 69
  The Secret Cocktail, 53
  White Lady, 169
El Diablo, 88
Emerald Gimlet, 144

F
fig preserves
  In the Bar with a Knife, 107
Filmograph, 30
Fog Cutter, 33
French 75, 149
Fright Night, 104
From the Depths, 176
Frostbite, 206

G

gin
  Arsenic and Old Lace, 20
  Blue Devil, 79
  Blue Moon, 138
  Corpse Reviver No. 2, 83
  Emerald Gimlet, 144
  Fog Cutter, 33
  French 75, 149
  Last Word, 40
  Martini, 111
  Monkey Gland, 46
  Moonlight, 152
  Negroni, 116
  Ramos Gin Fizz, 69
  Satan's Whiskers, 96
  The Secret Cocktail, 53
  Silver Bullet, 155
  Southside, 127
  Suffering Bastard, 57
  Summertime, 130
  White Lady, 169
ginger, fresh
  Wassail, 217
ginger ale
  Horses' Neck, 39
  Sleepyhead, 124
ginger beer
  Dark 'n' Stormy, 29
  El Diablo, 88
  Suffering Bastard, 57
Gochujang Caramel
  recipe, 186
  Ritual Visions, 186
Gold Rush, 74
Grand Marnier
  Satan's Whiskers, 96
grapefruit juice
  Don's Mix, 170
  labeling, 13
  Moonlight, 152
  Zombie, 170
grenadine
  Blood Orange Cooler, 175
  Monkey Gland, 46
  Scofflaw, 123
  The Secret Cocktail, 53
  Zombie, 170

H
half-and-half
  Eggnog, 205
Hell Cocktail, 91
home bar, about, 8–9
honey syrup
  Gold Rush, 74
  Hot Toddy, 210
Horror Hotel, 34
horseradish
  Bloody Mary, 23
Horses' Neck, 39

Hot Buttered Rum, 209
hot sauce
  Bloody Mary, 23
Hot Toddy, 210
Hpnotiq
  One Single Tear, 119
Hurricane, 66

I
In the Bar with a Knife, 107
Irish Coffee, 213

J
Jack-O'-Lantern Syrup
  Pumpkin Spice and Everything
  Nice, 214

K
Kirschwasser
  Moonlight, 152
  Virgin's Prayer, 58
kola tonic
  Filmograph, 30
Kümmel
  Silver Bullet, 155

L
large batches, 11
Last Word, 40
lavender bitters
  Ursula, 166
lead in glassware, 13
lemon
  Sangria, 95
lemon juice
  Alabazam, 19
  Bloody Mary, 23
  Blue Devil, 79
  Blue Moon, 138
  Charles Dickens's Punch, 202
  Corpse Reviver No. 2, 83
  From the Depths, 176
  Devil's Cocktail, 87
  Filmograph, 30
  Fog Cutter, 33
  French 75, 149
  Gold Rush, 74
  Hot Toddy, 210
  Hurricane, 66
  Midori Sour, 112
  One Single Tear, 119
  Ramos Gin Fizz, 69
  Ritual Visions, 186
  The Secret Cocktail, 53
  Silver Bullet, 155
  Sleepyhead, 124
  Summertime, 130
  Telltale Heart, 189
  White Lady, 169
Lemon Oleo Saccharum

  Chatham Artillery Punch, 65
  recipe, 65
lemon peel
  Charles Dickens's Punch, 202
lemon soda water
  Nightmare Tonic, 182
Licor 43
  Carajillo, 199
Life Everlasting Tincture
  One Single Tear, 119
Lillet Blanc
  Corpse Reviver No. 2, 83
lime juice
  Almas Perdidas, 137
  Dark 'n' Stormy, 29
  El Diablo, 88
  Emerald Gimlet, 144
  Fright Night, 104
  Last Word, 40
  (Midnight) Margaritas, 43
  Midori Sour, 112
  Obsidian Butterfly, 49
  Ramos Gin Fizz, 69
  Scofflaw, 123
  Southside, 127
  Suffering Bastard, 57
  Zombie, 170
lime soda water
  Nightmare Tonic, 182

M
Manhattan, 108
maple syrup
  Nightmare Tonic, 182
maraschino liqueur
  Blue Devil, 79
  Last Word, 40
  Virgin's Prayer, 58
Martini, 111
melon liqueur
  Midori Sour, 112
mezcal
  In the Bar with a Knife, 107
  Chupacabra, 143
  Horror Hotel, 34
  See also tequila
(Midnight) Margaritas, 43
Midori Sour, 112
milk
  Eggnog, 205
  Milk (Punch), 115
mint
  From the Depths, 176
  One Single Tear, 119
  Sleepyhead, 124
  Southside, 127
Monkey Gland, 46
Moonlight, 152
Mulled Cider, 179

220   **SPOOKY COCKTAILS**

N

Negroni, 116
Nightmare Tonic, 182

O

Obsidian Butterfly, 49
One Single Tear, 119
orange bitters
    Martini, 111
    Revolver, 92
    Satan's Whiskers, 96
    Scofflaw, 123
    Suburban, 54
    Telltale Heart, 189
orange flower water
    Ramos Gin Fizz, 69
orange juice
    Blood Orange Cooler, 175
    Monkey Gland, 46
    Painkiller, 120
    Sangria, 95
    Satan's Whiskers, 96
orange liqueur
    Corpse Reviver No. 2, 83
    (Midnight) Margaritas, 43
    White Lady, 169
orange twist
    Café Brulot, 195
oranges
    Mulled Cider, 179
    Sangria, 95
orgeat
    Fog Cutter, 33

P

Painkiller, 120
passion fruit syrup/puree
    Hurricane, 66
Peychaud's Bitters
    Sazerac, 70
    Vieux Carré, 73
pineapple juice
    Painkiller, 120
pomegranate juice
    Nightmare Tonic, 182
    Telltale Heart, 189
Popcorn-Washed Rum
    Fright Night, 104
    recipe, 104
port
    Devil's Cocktail, 87
    Suburban, 54
Pumpkin Juice, 185
Pumpkin Spice and Everything
    Nice, 214
Pumpkin Spice Simple Syrup
    Pumpkin Juice, 185
    recipe, 185
pumpkin/pumpkin puree
    Pumpkin Juice, 185

Pumpkin Spice and Everything
    Nice, 214
Pumpkin Spice Syrup, 214

R

Ramos Gin Fizz, 69
raspberry syrup, blue
    From the Depths, 176
Revolver, 92
Ritual Visions, 186
rum
    Charles Dickens's Punch, 202
    Chatham Artillery Punch, 65
    Dark 'n' Stormy, 29
    Eggnog, 205
    Fog Cutter, 33
    Fright Night, 104
    Hot Buttered Rum, 209
    Hurricane, 66
    Milk (Punch), 115
    Painkiller, 120
    Popcorn-Washed Rum, 104
    Suburban, 54
    Zombie, 170
rum, spiced
    Pumpkin Spice and Everything
    Nice, 214
rye whiskey
    Sazerac, 70
    Scofflaw, 123
    Suburban, 54
    Vieux Carré, 73

S

safety tips, 13
Saline Solution
    Ritual Visions, 186
Sangria, 95
Satan's Whiskers, 96
Sazerac, 70
Scofflaw, 123
Scotch whisky
    Scotch Mist, 50
Secret Cocktail, The, 53
sherry
    Fog Cutter, 33
    Obsidian Butterfly, 49
Silver Bullet, 155
Simple Syrup
    Alabazam, 19
    Blue Devil, 79
    Emerald Gimlet, 144
    Filmograph, 30
    French 75, 149
    Milk (Punch), 115
    Monkey Gland, 46
    Pumpkin Spice Simple Syrup, 185
    Ramos Gin Fizz, 69
    recipe, 19
    Sangria, 95

Sazerac, 70
Scofflaw, 123
The Secret Cocktail, 53
Silver Bullet, 155
Southside, 127
Summertime, 130
Telltale Heart, 189
Watermelon Cordial, 137
White Lady, 169
Sleepyhead, 124
smoking drinks, 13
Snakebite, 156
sotol
    Almas Perdidas, 137
Southside, 127
squid ink
    as coloring agent, 13
    Obsidian Butterfly, 49
Stinger, 161
strawberries
    Telltale Heart, 189
Suburban, 54
Suffering Bastard, 57
Summertime, 130
Suze
    Chupacabra, 143

T

tea, black
    Charles Dickens's Punch, 202
Telltale Heart, 189
tequila
    Chupacabra, 143
    El Diablo, 88
    Frostbite, 206
    (Midnight) Margaritas, 43
    Obsidian Butterfly, 49
    See also mezcal
tomato juice
    Bloody Mary, 23
troubleshooting, 12

U

ube extract
    Ursula, 166
Ursula, 166

V

vanilla extract
    Blood Orange Cooler, 175
Velvet Falernum
    Zombie, 170
vermouth, bitter
    Horror Hotel, 34
vermouth, blanco
    Chupacabra, 143
vermouth, dry
    Arsenic and Old Lace, 20
    In the Bar with a Knife, 107
    Chrysanthemum, 26

Martini, 111
    Satan's Whiskers, 96
    Scofflaw, 123
vermouth, sweet
    Americano, 103
    Corpse Reviver No. 1, 80
    Devil's Cocktail, 87
    Manhattan, 108
    Negroni, 116
    Satan's Whiskers, 96
    Vieux Carré, 73
Vieux Carré, 73
Virgin's Prayer, 58
vodka
    Bloody Mary, 23
    Midori Sour, 112
    One Single Tear, 119
    Ursula, 166

W

Wassail, 217
Watermelon Cordial
    Almas Perdidas, 137
    recipe, 137
whiskey, Irish
    Irish Coffee, 213
    See also bourbon; rye whiskey;
    Scotch whisky
whiskey, non-alcoholic
    Ritual Visions, 186
whiskey barrel-aged bitters
    Horror Hotel, 34
White Lady, 169
wine, red
    Sangria, 95
wine, white
    Moonlight, 152
Worcestershire sauce
    Bloody Mary, 23

Y

yogurt soda
    Ursula, 166

Z

Zombie, 170

ACKNOWLEDGEMENTS

Writing a cocktail book is no joke. It took me five years between *Romantic Cocktails* and this project to find the right time, right topic, and right place to do it again. Even with the perfect set of circumstances, no book happens in a vacuum.

This book is specifically for Stephen and our girls. This project could not have happened without your love, extra dog walks, confidence, occasional coaching, encyclopedic knowledge of horror movies, and cooking, especially while you were finishing up residency. I am a better writer and more interesting human because of you. Nikki and Tessie, continue being cuddle monsters, please.

To be honest, this book would not have been possible without the support and incredible knowledge from the bar community. Though I have not regularly held bar shifts since COVID lockdown started, the remarkable generosity of those I met in my seven years in the industry continues. Y'all are, now and forever, the MVPs of every cocktail book.

Family, thank you for your excitement about this project and cheering it on from the sidelines.

To anyone who fielded frantic requests for obscure cocktail ingredients with grace and kindness, thank you. Clay and Colleen, you're amazing.

This book likely would not have been finished if not for the wonderful friends who put up with me during my writing process. It is a lot, but it's here! Isabel, Ash, Ashlee, Soumya, Kirsten, Kelly, Emily, Cass, Kelly, Lia, Ashley, you have been more patient than I deserve.

Spooky Cocktails would never have come together if it was not for the work of my editor, Lindy Pokorny, publisher John Whalen and Cider Mill Press, rock star designer Steve Cooley, proofreader Jennifer Gott, and the wonder photography duo Alejandra and Jamie from Off The Line.

ABOUT THE AUTHOR

Clair McLafferty is a bartender turned data scientist based in Charlotte, North Carolina, where she lives with her husband and two dogs. In 2013, she quit her office job to make craft cocktails after writing about the local scene for two years. Making drinks fed into researching them, and hundreds of articles for publications including *The Washington Post*, *PUNCH*, and *The Food Network* followed. She is also the author of *The Classic & Craft Cocktail Recipe Book: The Definitive Guide to Mixing Perfect Cocktails from Aviation to Zombie* (Rockridge Press, 2017) and *Romantic Cocktails* (Whalen Book Works, 2019). For more of her writing, visit clairmclafferty.com.

ABOUT CIDER MILL PRESS
BOOK PUBLISHERS

Good ideas ripen with time. From seed to harvest, Cider Mill Press brings fine reading, information, and entertainment together between the covers of its creatively crafted books. Our Cider Mill bears fruit twice a year, publishing a new crop of titles each spring and fall.

"Where Good Books Are Ready for Press"

501 Nelson Place
Nashville, Tennessee 37214

cidermillpress.com